Dear Pat!
I enjoy being with you so
much I realy enjoy our
walk together
God bless you like you bless
muy life Jeremiah,

Pat
_____

From:

Angela
_____

Date:

6 - 29 - 2021
_____

Draw Near to

God

100 Bible Verses to Deepen Your Faith

ZONDERVAN®

1

You will seek Me
and find Me, when
you search for Me
with all your heart.

JEREMIAH 29:13

It's astonishing to ponder the reality that God invites us into relationship. From Genesis to Revelation, the Bible reveals God's desire for His people to know Him. But in all relationships, there must be intentionality in order for intimacy to thrive. A close relationship with God doesn't happen by chance. The words of the prophet Jeremiah convey the truth that we won't know God intimately unless we are serious about pursuing fellowship with Him. The phrase "search for Me with all your heart" (Jeremiah 29:13) indicates we'll need to devote time, focus, and energy to knowing God well. The primary ways we experience a flourishing relationship with the Lord are through Bible study, prayer, and worship. Spiritual disciplines are not intended to be approached with the mind-set of trying to earn favor with God. Instead they are the path to His grace, putting us in a posture to learn about God and to experience a vibrant relationship with Him.

> *Father, teach me to seek You with all my heart. Please give me a desire to know You and to make my relationship with You the most important thing in my life.*

2

If you seek
[understanding] as silver,
And search for her as
for hidden treasures;
Then you will
understand the
fear of the LORD,
And find the
knowledge of God.

PROVERBS 2:4–5

It's impossible for us to love God without knowing Him, and the best way to know Him is through the Scriptures. Thankfully, the Bible provides us with all the knowledge we need about God. But the Bible shouldn't be approached like a textbook. Attaining knowledge of God isn't like taking a history or math class where our motivation is to acquire information we will regurgitate on a test. The goal isn't for us to know *about* God but rather to *know* God. The writer of Proverbs instructs us to look for understanding "as silver, and search for her as for hidden treasures" (Proverbs 2:4–5). But like most things of value, this takes time. As we linger in the Scriptures seeking to understand His ways, character, and will through the holy Writ, we will come away with spiritual treasures. As we continue to mine the Word of God, those treasures will become the most valuable things in our life.

Lord, as I study Your Word, I pray You will increase my understanding and knowledge of You. I ask for the privilege of knowing You well and experiencing a vibrant relationship with You.

3

How precious also are Your
thoughts to me, O God!
How great is the sum of them!
If I should count them,
they would be more in
number than the sand;
When I awake, I am
still with You.

PSALM 139:17–18

*I*s there anyone in your life who knows everything about you and loves you anyway? When King David wrote Psalm 139, he emphasized God's complete knowledge of him. He wrote, "O LORD, You have searched me and known me. You know my sitting down and my rising up; You understand my thought afar off" (Psalm 139:1–2). God is omniscient, meaning He possesses infinite understanding and knows everything about His creation. It's both humbling and exhilarating when we realize God knows our darkest secrets, and He still pursues us. Amazingly, He also reveals Himself to us, so we have the opportunity to know Him. When we read the Scriptures, we ingest the very thoughts and words of God. King David marveled, "How precious also are Your thoughts to me, O God! How great is the sum of them!" (v. 17). God is infinite and will always have new things to reveal to us, and He will never reject us.

Father, You know everything about me and still love me. Thank You for the opportunity to have a relationship with You and enjoy Your fellowship.

4

Submit to God. Resist
the devil and he will
flee from you. Draw
near to God and He
will draw near to you.

JAMES 4:7–8

$\mathcal{A}$s followers of Jesus Christ, we can be as close to God as we choose to be. James instructed his readers, "Draw near to God and He will draw near to you." But close fellowship with God calls for submission to Him in every area of our lives. We can't walk closely with Christ and simultaneously harbor our pet sins. Jesus said, "If you love Me, keep My commandments" (John 14:15). The Enemy is committed to tempting us with sin that will wreak havoc on our fellowship with God. When that tactic doesn't work, Satan specializes in distracting us with the goal of luring us away from a pure devotion to Christ (2 Corinthians 11:3). But the apostle James insists that if we resist the Devil, he will flee. The primary way we resist the Enemy is by obeying God and drawing near to Him. There is nothing this world has to offer that is worth forfeiting our fellowship with the Lord.

> *Father, please help me submit to You and resist the Devil. I pray You will reveal the behaviors in me that You find offensive and lead me on Your paths of righteousness.*

5

Where can I go from
Your Spirit?
Or where can I flee from
Your presence? . . .
If I take the wings
of the morning,
And dwell in the uttermost
parts of the sea,
Even there Your hand
shall lead me,
And Your right hand
shall hold me.

PSALM 139:7, 9–10

If you were walking through a dangerous or unfamiliar territory, you would prefer a guide to come along who is familiar with the terrain. A guide provides direction, informs you of potential dangers, and keeps you on the right track. The same is true in life. Regardless of where we go or what we do, we will never find ourselves outside the presence of God. David marveled at this truth: "Where can I go from Your Spirit? Or where can I flee from Your presence?" (Psalm 139:7). God is always with us, and He longs to direct our steps. Yes, there are times when there seems to be no clear path. But the Scriptures promise that God guides His people, and when we get offtrack, He redirects our way. The psalmist wrote, "The steps of a good man are ordered by the Lord, and He delights in his way. Though he fall, he shall not be utterly cast down; for the Lord upholds him with His hand" (Psalm 37:23–24).

Father, I seek Your counsel and guidance in every aspect of my life. Lead me in Your ways and show me how You want me to live. I pray my life will bring glory to You.

6

This is the confidence
that we have in Him,
that if we ask anything
according to His will,
He hears us. And if we
know that He hears
us, whatever we ask,
we know that we have
the petitions that we
have asked of Him.

1 JOHN 5:14–15

Have you ever shared something deeply important and then realized the person you are speaking to isn't even listening? It's frustrating when we communicate what's on our heart and mind only to be ignored. The good news is God always hears our prayers. The apostle John assured his readers that if we ask anything that is according to God's will, He hears us. How do we know God's will? Through the Scriptures. Every promise God has made to His people reveals His will for us. So when we pray in alignment with His promises, we can be certain we are praying His will. Although there are times when we might not be sure if a specific situation is the will of God or not, we can always be confident He will hear us, and He will do what is good and right and best for us (Romans 8:28). As our relationship with God deepens and matures, we will want only the things He wants us to have, and we will be motivated to ask for those things that bring glory to Him.

Lord, thank You for hearing my prayers. Please reveal Your will for my life. Lead me to pray in alignment with Your will and to long for the same things You desire.

_7_

"Now, therefore,"
says the LORD,
"Turn to Me with
all your heart,
With fasting, with
weeping, and with
mourning."

JOEL 2:12

n the Old Testament, the nation of Israel repeatedly turned its back on God. In the book of Joel, Israel experienced a time of national calamity as a result of God's discipline. But even after Israel's disobedience, God called the nation to repent and return to Him. He does the same with us. When sin lures us away from God, we lose the fellowship we are intended to experience with Him. But God beckons us back to fellowship. No matter how far we've strayed, we can be confident that God will embrace us if we return to Him. His grace is stronger than even our most heinous sins. The prophet Joel instructed his audience to return with fasting, weeping, and mourning. In other words, they needed to repent and demonstrate remorse for their sins. God is full of grace and lovingly embraces the prodigals who return home, but He also calls for His people to repent of sin.

> *Lord, be quick to convict me of sins that impact my fellowship with You. Make me readily willing to repent of sin, and create in me a strong desire to obey You.*

8

I will meditate on the
glorious splendor
of Your majesty,
And on Your
wondrous works.

PSALM 145:5

*O*ur thought life is important, so it's not surprising that the Bible has a lot to say about managing our minds. For better or worse, the things we think about influence our life. Our minds are seldom quiet; we are always thinking about something. The good news is we have the ability to choose what we dwell on. King David resolved that he would think about or "meditate" on the Lord's majesty and wondrous works. To *meditate* on something means to turn it over and over in our mind, contemplating the topic from several different angles. Practically speaking, if we know how to worry, we already know how to meditate. But unlike worry, meditation has the potential to direct our thoughts onto the positive aspects of God's nature and power. When we meditate on all the ways God has worked on our behalf, it will stir our faith and increase our confidence that He will come through for us in the future.

Lord, I pray You will teach me to manage my mind. Help me to replace worry with thoughts that focus on Your promises and all the ways You have been faithful.

9

Put on the whole armor
of God, that you may
be able to stand against
the wiles of the devil.
For we do not wrestle
against flesh and blood,
but . . . against spiritual
hosts of wickedness in
the heavenly places.

EPHESIANS 6:11–12

*I*t's crucial we learn how to deal with the Enemy. In Ephesians 6, the apostle Paul instructed his readers about the resources available to every believer. The Greek word used for "whole armor" is *panoplia*, which refers to the equipment of a well-armed soldier.[1] Paul described both shields and weapons that aid believers in our struggles with the Devil. Satan's artillery draws from the spiritual forces of evil, so it's not surprising the weapons of our warfare are spiritual as well. As Christ-followers, we must remain alert and equip ourselves with the full armor of God. If we ignore the threats of the Enemy, we will be an easy target. Satan harasses God's people and causes an enormous amount of problems, but there is no reason for us to live in fear. God promises to guard against the evil one (Colossians 2:15; 2 Thessalonians 3:3). Still, we must do our part in being aware of Satan's schemes and actively trust Christ to defend us.

> *Lord, help me to be mindful of the Enemy's schemes and his desire to distract me from my devotion to Christ. Teach me to equip myself with Your armor.*

10

Then Peter said to them, "Repent, and let every one of you be baptized in the name of Jesus Christ for the remission of sins; and you shall receive the gift of the Holy Spirit."

ACTS 2:38

od's gift of salvation is for those of us who place our faith in the finished work of Jesus Christ and repent of our sins. Over and over, the Scriptures demonstrate that God longs to have a relationship with His people, but because of our sinful nature, it's not possible to be reconciled to the Father apart from saving faith in Jesus Christ. In the early church, Peter taught that Christ-followers are to repent from their sins and be baptized. To "repent" means to have a heartfelt sorrow for sin and a sincere commitment to forsake it and walk in obedience to Christ.[2] Baptism doesn't have the ability to save people from their sins but rather is an outward expression of inward faith in Christ. Authentic salvation will always be accompanied by repentance and a willingness to identify with the body of believers who confess Christ as their Savior.

> Lord, I praise You for the gift of salvation. Please forgive me for the wrongs I have done You and lead me in a life that ever turns away from sin.

11

"I will be a Father
to you,
And you shall be My
sons and daughters,
Says the Lord Almighty."

2 CORINTHIANS 6:18

No matter our age, human beings never outgrow the need to be parented. Some of us come from homes with excellent parents, while others of us grow up with absentee or abusive parents. Regardless of our parental history, God longs to father us. Even the best-intentioned parents make mistakes while raising children because, as humans, we are all flawed. But God is the perfect parent. He is both provisional and practical. As a loving Father, He meets our needs and is faithful to guide, protect, and discipline His children. The New Testament teaches we are adopted as sons and daughters through Jesus Christ (Ephesians 1:5). Adoption is an intentional act that requires forethought from the adoptive parent. The Scriptures make it clear that God embraces the role of Father and that He chose us before the foundation of the world to be His children (vv. 4–5). Every child of God has the opportunity to be parented by a loving Father who wants the best for His children.

Father, I ask You to parent me. I pray for Your guidance, counsel, provision, and protection. I want to know You as my loving and faithful Father.

12

"He who has My commandments and keeps them, it is he who loves Me. And he who loves Me will be loved by My Father, and I will love him and manifest Myself to him."

JOHN 14:21

There is a dramatic difference between *loving* Jesus and *behaving* for Jesus. In the New Testament, the Pharisees clearly demonstrated that it's possible to be a rule-keeper and yet have no real love for God (Matthew 15:8). In those kinds of instances, the motivation to obey is fueled by societal pressure or fear of disappointing. But when no one is looking, there is a desire to rebel. If we truly love Jesus, we will *want* to keep His commands because our desire is to please Him. The more we mature spiritually, the more we understand that His rules aren't intended to limit us, but rather to keep us from harm. If God forbids something, it's not because He is keeping something from us; rather, the things He forbids have the potential to destroy us. It's not only our obedience but also our motivation for obeying Christ that matters to God. It's the difference between dry religion and a vibrant relationship. Religion is motivated by rules, but relationships are fueled by love.

> Lord, please give me a heart that loves You above all things. I pray for a strong desire to obey Your commandments and for a keen sense of Your love.

13

But it is good for me
to draw near to God;
I have put my trust
in the Lord GOD,
That I may declare
all Your works.

PSALM 73:28

*I*t's common to want to talk about things that bring us joy. When someone or something is important to us, we adjust our lives so we can devote as much time as possible to those people and things that bring us satisfaction. The psalmist said, "But it is good for me to draw near to God; I have put my trust in the Lord GOD" (Psalm 73:28). Clearly the writer had determined he wanted to live in close fellowship with God. It was an intentional decision and not mere happenstance. Earlier, the psalmist admitted to having struggled and nearly succumbed to the temptations of the wicked, but then he chose to seek refuge in God's care (vv. 2–3, 28). As a result, he enjoyed companionship with the Lord and was able to witness God's works. His natural inclination, then, was to share what God had done. As our history with God grows, we too will see Him act in ways that bring us such delight that we won't be able to keep ourselves from sharing His goodness with the world.

Father, like the psalmist, I long to draw near to You. I want to live in such close fellowship with You that I will have a natural desire to tell of Your wonderous works.

_14_

"The thief does not come except to steal, and to kill, and to destroy. I have come that they may have life, and that they may have it more abundantly."

JOHN 10:10

God has a good plan for every one of His children, but the Enemy has a blueprint for our destruction. In the Scriptures, one of the most well-known names for Jesus is the "good shepherd" (John 10:11). In biblical times, the role of a shepherd was widely known, and it was common knowledge that sheep were vulnerable animals who were prone to wander, stubborn, and in need of constant redirection from the shepherd in order to survive. In the ancient Near East, it was typical for a shepherd to walk ahead of his sheep to make sure predators wouldn't invade the flock. The shepherd protected and provided for his flock, sometimes even at the expense of his own life (v. 11). In the same way, Jesus watches over us as a shepherd protects his sheep. Satan's desire is to inflict destruction, suffering, and loss, but Jesus came so we could have abundant life.

Lord, I pray I will live the abundant life You intend for me to have. Guard me from the plan of the Enemy to wreak havoc in my life. Jesus, thank You for being my Good Shepherd.

15

But God demonstrates
His own love toward
us, in that while we
were still sinners,
Christ died for us.

ROMANS 5:8

*I*n the garden of Eden, Adam and Eve experienced perfect fellowship with God and one another. But Paradise was shattered when they succumbed to the temptation of the Enemy and ate from the Tree of Knowledge of Good and Evil (Genesis 3:3–6). God had warned them that if they ate from the tree, they would die (2:17). But Satan convinced them they were missing out, so they disobeyed God and ate the forbidden fruit. As a result, sin infected not just Adam and Eve but the entire human race, and fellowship with God was broken. Yet God spared nothing in His redemptive plan, not even His own Son. *While we were still sinners*, God initiated the plan of salvation; Jesus died on the cross on our behalf so we might be reconciled to the Father. There can be no greater demonstration of love than God's willingness to sacrifice His only Son and Jesus' willingness to obey His Father. Our redemption was no small thing. The plan was costly, and it was motivated by love.

> *Father, thank You for loving me while I was still a sinner. I praise You for Your redemptive plan of salvation. Teach me to love others unconditionally, just as You've loved me.*

16

Delight yourself
also in the LORD,
And He shall give
you the desires
of your heart.

PSALM 37:4

*K*ing David understood the sheer delight a believer can experience in his or her relationship with God. David was, after all, a man after God's own heart, and it was he who penned the words, "Oh, taste and see that the LORD is good" (Psalm 34:8). When God is our greatest treasure, our desires begin to align with His will, and our goal is to bring Him glory. We come to love the things He loves and to hate the things He hates. Those things we once thought we couldn't live without become irrelevant, while other things we used to give no thought to become central to our lives. Our hearts are designed to be filled with the love of God, and anything less is a cheap imitation. When we delight in the Lord, He is quick to give us the desires of our heart because those desires have become the very things He wants us to have.

Lord, I long to desire You above all things. Shape my goals and dreams so that they align with Your will and so that I will live a life that brings You glory.

17

Do not love the world
or the things in the
world. If anyone loves
the world, the love of
the Father is not in him.

1 JOHN 2:15

In the Bible, "the world" often refers to things that are contrary to the ways of God. The Scriptures warn we must choose whether we want to have a friendship with the world or a friendship with God. The apostle James wrote, "Adulterers and adulteresses! Do you not know that friendship with the world is enmity with God? Whoever therefore wants to be a friend of the world makes himself an enemy of God" (James 4:4). As Christians, we are called to have allegiance to God's kingdom and reject the rebellious ways of the world that disregard the Lord. Of course, that doesn't mean we shouldn't be kind to all people and show respect to those we disagree with. It simply means that as followers of Christ, we live by biblical standards rather than blending in with the ways of secular society. And as our love for God increases, the enticements of the world will grow increasingly dim.

Father, please teach my heart to be fully devoted to You. Give me both a strong desire to please You and the strength to forsake the lures of this world.

18

Let us know,
Let us pursue the
knowledge of the Lord.
His going forth
is established as
the morning;
He will come to
us like the rain.

HOSEA 6:3

The prophet Hosea cast a compelling vision for God's people when he wrote, "Let us pursue the knowledge of the LORD" (Hosea 6:3). God's people had strayed and were unrepentant in regard to their sin, so God inflicted Israel with divine judgment (5:4–6). Rather than seeking God for deliverance, they looked to Assyria for healing (5:13).[3] Hosea beckoned God's people to return to the Lord: "Come, and let us return to the LORD; for He has torn, but He will heal us" (6:1). Hosea understood that after a time of rebellion, the wise thing for God's people to do was humbly submit to His discipline. Though they had grievously sinned, they were not beyond God's grace and restoration. Thankfully, neither are we. When we sin, the wise thing to do is humbly confess our sin and seek God's forgiveness. It's far better to be disciplined by the Lord and restored to fellowship with Him than to continue in evil and separation from Him.

> *Father, I pray that You would reveal the sins of my life to me and help me to repent of them. Please forgive me for the times I have sought refuge in the people and things of this world, rather than in You.*

19

"Blessed are those
who hunger and thirst
for righteousness,
For they shall be filled."

MATTHEW 5:6

S piritually speaking, desperation is a gift. It's usually only after we've exhausted all of our resources and come up empty that we realize how desperately we need God. Each of us was created with needs only God can meet, but we oftentimes try to fill those voids with worldly resources. Until we realize that God is the only thing that can satisfy, we will continue in idolatry. When Jesus preached the Sermon on the Mount, He said, "Blessed are those who hunger and thirst for righteousness, for they shall be filled" (Matthew 5:6). To "hunger and thirst for righteousness" means to possess a desire to be free from sin and be in right relationship with God.[4] Simply put, it's a desire to be holy. The person who hungers and thirsts for righteousness would rather have God than anything else. Jesus promises they will be filled.

> *Father, I seek contentment in Christ. Please give me wisdom that prevents me from seeking contentment in the things of this world. Increase my thirst for You, as I claim Your promise to satisfy that thirst.*

20

Just as you received
Christ Jesus as Lord,
continue to live
your lives in him.

COLOSSIANS 2:6 NIV

When Paul wrote his letter to the church at Colossae, he warned the Colossians not to be led astray by deceptive teaching (Colossians 2:4–8). False teaching was rampant in Colossae and had infiltrated the church. Although Paul couldn't be present with the church physically, he cared immensely for the believers there and sought to minister to them. In his letter, Paul directed the believers back to the foundational teaching they learned when they first became Christians. "Just as you received Christ Jesus as Lord," he instructed, "continue to live your lives in him" (v. 6). At the core of this message is the fact that Jesus *is* Lord, and His believers are to continue moving forward with that truth as the basis of our belief system. Practically speaking, that means we approach our day-to-day lives in light of Jesus' lordship and manage our affairs in submission to Him. Obedience to Christ as Lord is not a one-time act but rather a daily devotion that continues throughout the span of our lives.

Father, I pray I will be led and taught by Your spirit of truth. Give me discernment to quickly spot deceptive teaching and courage to live in submission to You.

21

Do not merely listen
to the word, and so
deceive yourselves.
Do what it says.

JAMES 1:22 NIV

*M*illions of people visit the doctor each year and are told that if they improve their diet and introduce exercise into their daily routine, they will avoid a variety of medical problems. Unfortunately, not everyone makes the necessary adjustments, and they suffer the consequences. In a similar way, the apostle James teaches it's not enough for Christians to hear the Word of God; we must be people who obey the Word. James wrote, "Do not merely listen to the word, and so deceive yourselves. Do what it says." Yes, hearing the Word of God is essential, but it's only the first step. To truly be children of God, we must obey the Scriptures, and if we don't, James says, we are deceived. But James goes on to reassure us that if we do, in fact, both hear *and* obey the Word, we will be blessed (James 1:25). That blessing, however, won't come from merely hearing; it's obedience that opens up the storehouses of heaven and rains down showers of blessings from God.

Father, I want to be both a hearer and a doer of Your Word. Guide me with Your Spirit to understand and obey Your holy Scriptures.

22

"I have loved you with
an everlasting love;
Therefore with
lovingkindness I
have drawn you."

JEREMIAH 31:3

H as someone ever made an important promise to you, but then wasn't able to keep it? It's devastating, isn't it? In Jeremiah 31, God promised a new covenant to His people (vv. 31–40). Leading up to that promise, God communicated to Israel that they would be His people, (vv. 1–14), that He would grant them mercy (vv. 15–26), and He would keep them safe (vv. 27–30). Time and again, Israel had rebelled against God. They had sought idols and disobeyed the Lord and were far from being worthy of God's kindness. So what motivated God to extend a new covenant? Undoubtedly, it was His love. Verse 3 says, "I have loved you with an everlasting love." It's difficult for us to wrap our minds around the magnitude of God's love, but He has a long and faithful history of demonstrating divine love to His people. Regardless of our past, God's love remains steadfast, and He is faithful to keep His promises.

> *Father, thank You for Your steadfast love and Your perfect track record of keeping Your promises. Fill me with an ever-present awareness of Your constant love and faithfulness.*

23

Finally, brothers and
sisters, whatever
is true, whatever is
noble, whatever is
right, whatever is pure,
whatever is lovely,
whatever is admirable—
if anything is excellent
or praiseworthy—think
about such things.

PHILIPPIANS 4:8 NIV

It's easy to fall into the trap of thinking about what "might happen." We worry and agonize and rehearse worst-case scenarios over and over in our minds until we have—sometimes literally—worried ourselves sick. To combat this and other poisonous thoughts, the apostle Paul encouraged his readers to think about what is "true" (Philippians 4:8). We have the ability to manage our thoughts. We can reject thoughts that are untrue or not in alignment with how a believer should think. When we are tempted to worry, we have the option of finding a pertinent scripture and meditating on the particular promise that speaks to our situation. The psalmist wrote, "I will meditate on your precepts and consider your ways" (Psalm 119:15 NIV). We don't have to be victims of negative thinking. Instead, Paul taught that we are capable of cultivating an excellent and praiseworthy thought life that will improve our quality of lives.

Father, teach me to reject those thoughts that aren't true and that aren't worthy of my time and energy. Help me to rein in my thoughts and focus on those things that are uplifting and pleasing to You.

24

Without faith it is impossible to please Him, for he who comes to God must believe that He is, and that He is a rewarder of those who diligently seek Him.

HEBREWS 11:6

It's safe to say most of us would like to grow in faith. After all, the Bible says without faith it's impossible to please God. It's notable that the disciples asked Jesus to "increase our faith" (Luke 17:5). The disciples weren't the only ones who petitioned Jesus for more faith. A father in desperate need of healing for his sick son said to Jesus, "Lord, I believe; help my unbelief!" (Mark 9:24). As we approach God, we must believe not only that He exists but that He will reward those who diligently seek Him. Knowing God rewards those who earnestly seek Him can serve as a motivation to persevere in our pursuit of God. The Scriptures reveal that Jesus is the "perfecter of faith," so like the disciples and the father with the sick son, we can approach Jesus with confidence and ask Him to increase our faith (Hebrews 12:2 NIV).

> *Lord, I pray You will continually increase my faith. Help me to identify areas of unbelief and replace them with the kind of faith that is powerful enough to move mountains.*

25

He is not far from
each one of us; for in
Him we live and move
and have our being.

ACTS 17:27–28

When the apostle Paul addressed the men of Athens, he noted that while they were very religious, it was apparent they were still searching for God. In an attempt to "cover all the bases," they'd even gone so far as to inscribe an altar to an unknown god (Acts 17:23). But the Bible teaches there is only one God, and He is eager to be found. When Paul said, "He is not far from each one of us," he was referring to the fact that God has revealed Himself to all people through the natural human conscience (Acts 17:27; Romans 2:14–15). God's revelation of Himself should serve as motivation for all people to seek Him. Even the Greek poets acknowledged the revelation of God in nature, though they wrongly attributed it to false gods. Paul referred to the Cretan poet Epimenides who said "for in Him we live and move and have our being."[5] The God of the Bible has made it possible for all people to know Him, but the only path to the Father is through Jesus His Son (John 14:6).

Father, thank You for Your plan of salvation. Because of Christ's sacrifice, I can be reconciled to You. I pray I will seek You with all my heart and enjoy eternal fellowship with You.

26

Commit your works
to the LORD,
And your thoughts
will be established.

PROVERBS 16:3

$\mathcal{A}$t some point, most of us have been guilty of making plans without first consulting God and *then* asking Him to bless our agenda. To us, our ways always seem right, but God knows our hearts, and He weighs our motives (Proverbs 16:1–2). The writer of Proverbs instructs his readers to "Commit your works to the LORD, and your thoughts will be established." This instruction draws from the preceding two verses that establish the fact that God assumes the ownership of His people's plans, and He alone can purify our motives.[6] When we entrust our plans to God's guidance, we don't have to worry about their effectiveness, because the outcome of our efforts is in God's hands. God can purify our motives. He can take our selfish ambitions and transform them into holy ambitions that are pleasing to Him and productive for the kingdom of God.

Father, teach me to seek Your guidance in every area of life. Please purify my motives, and turn my ambitions away from my own selfish desires and toward Your holy plan.

27

"I have given them the glory that you gave me, that they may be one as we are one—I in them and you in me—so that they may be brought to complete unity. Then the world will know that you sent me and have loved them even as you have loved me."

JOHN 17:22–23 NIV

*I*t's staggering to contemplate that just before going to the cross Jesus took time to pray not only for His disciples but for all future believers (John 17:20). In the High Priestly Prayer, Jesus prayed to the Father, "I have given them the glory that you gave me, that they be one as we are one—I in them and you in me—so that they may be brought to complete unity." Even as the horrors of Calvary drew near, Jesus' thoughts focused on the unity of His church. Jesus prayed that all believers would be so unified that it would be evident even to unbelievers. The love Christians have for one another and the desire to share the gospel should be readily apparent to the outside world. Through the unity we share with our brothers and sisters in Christ, we demonstrate to a watching world that God loves His people just as He loves Jesus.

Father, let there be unity in Christ's church. Please empower me to love my brothers and sisters in Christ, as Your Word commands.

28

The kingdom of God is
not eating and drinking,
but righteousness
and peace and joy
in the Holy Spirit.

ROMANS 14:17

*I*n first-century Christianity, the early church experienced confusion about what was appropriate behavior. When Paul wrote Romans 14, he addressed whether Christians needed to adhere to Jewish dietary laws. Theologically, Paul sided with the "strong" who didn't see any need to follow those laws, but at the same time, he encouraged them not to be unsympathetic to the "weak" who still felt compelled to follow the Jewish dietary laws (Romans 14:1–16). Paul reminded his audience of what matters most: "The kingdom of God is not eating and drinking, but righteousness and peace and joy in the Holy Spirit." In other words, Paul emphasized that the kingdom of God is not about enjoying specific freedoms but rather embracing the peace, joy, and righteousness to be found in the Holy Spirit. The point of the Christian's life is not to be offended when a "weaker" Christian insists on a particular way of worship. The point is for the stronger to defer to the weaker out of love.

> *Father, please help me walk in love with those who are both stronger and weaker in their faith than me. Lead me by Your Holy Spirit so that I do Your will and defer to others out of love.*

29

The LORD your God
in your midst,
The Mighty One, will save;
He will rejoice over
you with gladness,
He will quiet you
with His love,
He will rejoice over
you with singing.

ZEPHANIAH 3:17

*H*ave you ever looked forward with anticipation to a specific day that was approaching? The theme in the book of Zephaniah is the "day of the LORD" (Zephaniah 1:7). This coming day reveals two aspects: one of judgment against those who reject God and one of blessing for those who follow Him.[7] As a nation, Judah had turned its back on its covenant obligations to God. Without repentance and God's mercy, Judah would face judgment. But God longed to restore Judah, just as He longs to restore today's believers who have wandered from the faith (3:11–13). Although Judah was weakened by its disobedience, God's presence did not leave them, and He was faithful to save them from their demise. Perhaps most remarkable is that even after Judah's disobedience, God still delighted in them—and, amazingly, He still delights in us. He rejoices over us with singing. God's faithful love and grace ever beckon the wayward back to His embrace.

> *Father, I pray I will be continually aware of Your love. Help me to understand that You truly delight in Your people—in me—and that Your grace beckons us to Your embrace.*

30

"No one can come
to Me unless the
Father who sent
Me draws him."

JOHN 6:44

Have you ever been courted by someone who was attempting to win your affection? It's flattering, isn't it? But the reality is that all people have been courted by God. Sadly, in our natural state, human beings have a desire for sin instead of God. Romans 3:11 says, "There is none who understands; there is none who seeks after God." The good news is that God seeks us. If we experience a desire to follow Jesus, it's because the Father has given us the inclination to do so. Jesus said, "No one can come to Me unless the Father who sent Me draws him." In His great love, God seeks to save each person from that natural state of sin and replace the coldness of hearts with a love for the Savior. But it is up to us to turn to Him and allow ourselves to be found.

> *Father, thank You for seeking me before I even had an inclination to draw near to You. Continually increase my desire for You, and make me thirst for the things of Your kingdom.*

31

You will show me
the path of life;
In Your presence is
fullness of joy;
At Your right hand are
pleasures forevermore.

PSALM 16:11

Oftentimes it's tempting to spend our time wanting and waiting for the next thing. But it's good to celebrate the blessings we already possess. In Psalm 16, King David communicated his gratitude for his relationship with God and the provision the Lord had given him (vv. 5–6). David was content in God and thoroughly enjoyed the blessings the Lord had bestowed on him. At the same time, David anticipated eternal life in God's presence, and he realized his best days were yet to come. Like David, we, too, were created to enjoy fellowship with God and find our contentment in Him. Yet, as believers in Jesus Christ, our best days are always ahead of us. We are free to celebrate the good gifts God has already given us all, knowing the best is still yet to come.

> *Father, thank You for all the ways You have blessed me. Help my heart to be content and my soul filled with gratitude to You. If I experience discontentment, let it only be because I want a closer relationship with You.*

32

The LORD. . . . will be
the sure foundation
for your times,
a rich store of
salvation and wisdom
and knowledge;
the fear of the LORD is
the key to this treasure.

ISAIAH 33:5–6 NIV

When the prophet Isaiah wrote Isaiah 33, Assyria had been attacking God's people and seemed to be getting away with it. But God came to the rescue of His people and provided everything they needed to persevere. Like the people of Zion, we as modern-day believers have come to know that life is uncertain. Some of us have experienced traumatic events. Even if we haven't experienced tragedy for ourselves, we know people whose lives have been changed in an instant. Some days just a casual glance at the news can make us feel as if the ground might well crumble under our feet. But God's people are not called to live with the burden of fear and anxiety. God is our constant source of stability, and He provides His people with wisdom and knowledge for every situation. When the world around us is changing and reeling out of control, we can rest assured that God never changes (Malachi 3:6). He is aware of everything and holds sovereign control over every circumstance (Luke 12:5–7).

Father, You are my constant source of stability. In times of uncertainty, help me remember You are always in control and have power over every circumstance.

33

Now by this we
know that we know
Him, if we keep His
commandments.

1 JOHN 2:3

nyone who has spent much time around a child has probably heard the question, "Why do I have to do this?" Kids are known for asking—often repeatedly—"Why?" They, along with most adults, are much more comfortable obeying a rule if they understand the reason behind it and if they trust the integrity of the authority figure issuing the rule. In the same way, the more a Christ-follower knows and trusts God, the more inclined he or she will be to keep His commands. Salvation, of course, is by grace through faith alone. It is not a result of works (Ephesians 2:8–9). But after we experience a personal and saving relationship with Jesus Christ, we will have an increased desire to please Him and, as a result, will keep His commands. Our obedience isn't the reason for our salvation, but it is evidence that we have experienced the saving grace and love of Christ Jesus.

> *Lord, open my heart to know You, and teach me to trust You, so that I will long to obey You.*

34

"Come to Me, all you who labor and are heavy laden, and I will give you rest. Take My yoke upon you and learn from Me, for I am gentle and lowly in heart, and you will find rest for your souls. For My yoke is easy and My burden is light."

MATTHEW 11:28–30

The stress of daily living and the pace of modern culture can be burdensome. Scores of people are overcommitted in their schedules and live with chronic fatigue that too easily turns to burnout. But Jesus invites us into an alternative way of living. "For My yoke is easy and My burden is light," He said. In the farm communities of Jesus' day, people understood that a yoke was used to link two farm animals together and then connect them to a plow to be pulled. A yoke didn't eliminate the work of pulling the plow, but it did divide it between the two animals so that one wasn't overburdened with the task. Likewise, all of us have a workload we are required to carry, but Jesus offers to come alongside and help us carry the burdens that are too much for us to handle on our own. We can trust Jesus with our burdens; He will lighten our load. And when we turn to Him for help, He promises we will find rest for our souls.

Lord, teach me to entrust my burdens—big and small—to Your care. Fill my life with the peace of knowing You are there to help me carry every load. I am so blessed to find rest in You.

35

Add to your faith virtue,
to virtue knowledge,
to knowledge self-
control, to self-control
perseverance, to
perseverance godliness,
to godliness brotherly
kindness, and to
brotherly kindness love.

2 PETER 1:5–7

The Christian life is designed to be a journey of spiritual growth. And while that growth is a result of God's grace, our participation is still required. Paul wrote, "Continue to work out your salvation with fear and trembling, for it is God who works in you to will and to act in order to fulfill his good purpose" (Philippians 2:12–13 NIV). It is true that God has given His people all we need to live godly lives, but we must apply ourselves and put ourselves in a posture to receive the means of grace that God uses to mature us.[8] Peter listed seven qualities of the godly life. Although the list isn't comprehensive, Peter explained that these are desirable characteristics that will keep us from becoming ineffective and unproductive. Like the fruit of the Spirit (Galatians 5:22–23), these characteristics are a result of a vibrant relationship with Jesus Christ. When we abide in Jesus, we bear fruit, and it becomes evident that we are, in fact, His disciples (John 15:5, 8).

Lord, as I continue in this journey of spiritual growth, please guide me to become the person You designed me to be.

36

"'And you shall love the LORD your God with all your heart, with all your soul, with all your mind, and with all your strength.' This is the first commandment. And the second, like it, is this: 'You shall love your neighbor as yourself.'"

MARK 12:30–31

*I*n the book of Mark, one of the scribes asked Jesus which of the commandments was the most important. Without hesitation, Jesus said, "'Love the Lord your God with all your heart, with all your soul, with all your mind, and with all your strength.' This is the first commandment. And the second, like it, is this: 'You shall love your neighbor as yourself.'" Jesus was quoting from passages in Deuteronomy and Leviticus that every Jew would have been familiar with. Together, these two commands sum up the Ten Commandments because the first four pertain to our relationship with God and the last six pertain to how we treat our fellow human beings. Although none of us have the ability to love perfectly, these two commands are at the core of the Christian faith. One of the most powerful prayers we can habitually offer up to God is to ask Him to give us a heart that loves Him above all things and that loves our neighbor as ourselves.

Father, Your Word says that without love I have nothing. Empower me to love You above all things and love others as Your Scriptures command.

37

"I was hungry and you
gave Me food; I was
thirsty and you gave Me
drink; I was a stranger
and you took Me in;
I was naked and you
clothed Me; I was sick
and you visited Me;
I was in prison and
you came to Me."

MATTHEW 25:35–36

*T*he Bible reveals that God cares deeply for the poor and afflicted. As Christians, we are to concern ourselves with the same things God cares about. It's no secret that God has a heart for the poor, and He calls His children to tend to their sufferings. In the book of Matthew, Jesus was speaking about the final judgment when believers will be separated from non-believers. One evidence of saving faith that will differentiate the saved from the lost is a history of caring for those in need. Our good deeds don't save us, but they are evidence of a genuine faith. If we understand how desperately poor in spirit we are apart from Christ, the inevitable result is we will sympathize and have compassion for the poor of this world. The more we come to understand the gospel, the more our hearts will relate to the poor and marginalized as we realize that apart from Christ we would spiritually be in the same condition.

> *God, break my heart over the things that break Your heart. Teach me to love all those whom You love and to serve all those You would have me to serve.*

38

I will instruct you
and teach you in the
way you should go;
I will counsel you with
my loving eye on you.

PSALM 32:8 NIV

*H*ave you ever wished you could be sure you were on the right path and making the right decisions? It's easy to second-guess our choices and wonder if somewhere along the way we got offtrack. Psalm 32 is most often regarded as a "thanksgiving hymn" in which God's people offer thanks for their sins being forgiven.[9] In addition to offering thanks for the forgiveness of sins, the psalmist—David—acknowledged his own transgressions to the Lord (Psalm 32:5–6). In verse 8, God responded to David's confession with this reassurance: "I will instruct you and teach you in the way you should go; I will counsel you with my loving eye on you" (NIV) At some point in our lives, we all make poor choices or unintentionally lose our way. But if we seek the Lord's guidance and ask for His forgiveness, He is faithful to forgive and to get us back on the right path.

Father, I want to make good choices that honor You. I pray You will instruct and teach me. Please redirect me when I need it, and provide assurance when I am on the right path.

39

"These things I have
spoken to you, that in
Me you may have peace.
In the world you will
have tribulation; but be
of good cheer, I have
overcome the world."

JOHN 16:33

*J*ohn 14–17 is a section of Scripture that theologians refer to as the "Farewell Discourse." At this point in the biblical narrative, Jesus is just hours from going to the cross, and these chapters record the last conversations Jesus had with His disciples before Calvary. Jesus knew His disciples were fearful, and He knew they didn't understand the magnitude of what was about to take place. Because He loved these followers, He wanted to prepare them for His physical absence. The truths Jesus spoke to those disciples apply to us as modern-day believers as well. Although we won't be faced with the horror of watching Christ walk the road to Golgotha, we will experience changes that will wound us and leave us reeling. So when Jesus said to His disciples, "in Me you may have peace," that promise was for us too. But notice that He said, "*in Me* you may have peace." There is no peace apart from Jesus. Yes, this world will send us troubles, but remember Jesus has already overcome the world.

Father, there is so much in this world I don't understand, but I pray for Your peace in every circumstance. In the midst of trouble, let it be Your peace that rules my heart.

40

"Fear not, for I
am with you;
Be not dismayed,
for I am your God.
I will strengthen you,
Yes, I will help you,
I will uphold you
with My righteous
right hand."

ISAIAH 41:10

*F*ear is a problem everyone deals with to some degree. For some of us, our greatest fear is being left to face our challenges alone. But God promises He will never abandon us. Over and over again, He reassures us of His presence and His intervention in our lives. Through the pen of the prophet Isaiah, God said, "Fear not, for I am with you." The sheer relief of knowing the almighty God is present with us in every situation should empower God's people to move forward with boldness. When we are up against circumstances that are too much for us, we can rely on His promise: "I will strengthen you, yes, I will help you, I will uphold you with My righteous right hand." The Christian life is not about mustering up enough strength to meet the demands of life. It is about walking with Jesus and trusting Him to provide the resources and strength we don't possess on our own, while continuing to move forward in faith to meets life's challenges.

Father, I don't want my life to be characterized by fear. Help me remember You are always with me, strengthening and encouraging. Replace my stress and anxiety with Your peace and purpose.

41

I am continually
with You;
You hold me by
my right hand.
You will guide me
with Your counsel,
And afterward
receive me to glory.

PSALM 73:23–24

*A*saph was a worship leader during the time that David was king of Israel (1 Chronicles 15:16–19). In Psalm 73, Asaph deals with the age-old problem of why the righteous suffer while the wicked seem to prosper. But rather than abandoning his faith, Asaph went to the sanctuary and worshiped (v. 17). He understood the role worship plays in realigning our thoughts, for when we commune with God, we are better able to see things in their proper perspective.[10] Asaph returned from the sanctuary with new clarity. He realized what he believed to be true about the prosperity of the wicked was only a pretense and not reality (vv. 17–18). Asaph came to understand that the Lord is present with every believer, offering His counsel, and when the time comes, He will guide us to glory. The wicked lack that blessing. In times of trouble, God is worthy of our worship. And that worship is also beneficial to us.

Father, You have given me every reason to worship You all the days of my life. I pray that in times of discouragement I will be quick to seek You and to offer my praise and worship to You.

42

Be anxious for nothing,
but in everything by
prayer and supplication,
with thanksgiving, let your
requests be made known
to God; and the peace of
God, which surpasses all
understanding, will guard
your hearts and minds
through Christ Jesus.

PHILIPPIANS 4:6–7

*W*orry has the ability to rob us of time, good health, a sound mind, and quality of life. The apostle Paul shared an effective prescription for worry. In his letter to the church at Philippi, Paul told his readers not to be anxious. Instead of worrying, he instructed them to pray, to offer thanks for the ways God had already blessed them, and to lay their requests before God. That same advice applies to believers today. How often do we worry ourselves sick and barely even bother to pray? What might our lives look like if we invested as much time in prayer as we waste in worry? Paul said the outcome of a prayerful life is peace that transcends the most difficult of situations and guards our hearts and minds. Jesus Himself warned that while worry is ineffective, prayer has the power to move mountains (Matthew 6:27; 17:20). Worry leads to a destination of turmoil, while prayer leads to peace.

> *Jesus, I need to have more self-discipline to devote myself to prayer. Just as the disciples asked You, I ask You to teach me how to pray, to entrust my worries to You.*

43

For the LORD God is
a sun and shield;
The LORD will give
grace and glory;
No good thing will
He withhold
From those who
walk uprightly.

PSALM 84:11

very good thing we possess comes from the hand of God. We might be tempted to believe that we are the masters of our fate and have worked hard to get where we are. And while it may be true that we've worked hard, it is God who has given us the strength to work, the opportunities to flourish, and the ability to complete our tasks. The psalmist understood that all favor and honor come from the Lord. He described God as "a sun and shield," meaning God is the source of all our light and protection. If we enjoy a measure of favor or honor, it's because God has allowed it. The apostle James described the same concept this way: "Every good and perfect gift is from above, coming down from the Father of the heavenly lights" (James 1:17 NIV). God's blessings are too many to number, but if we are mindful of His providence, we will begin to see His hand in those blessings everywhere we look.

Lord, You have given me every good thing I possess. You have poured out Your grace on me time and again. You are my provision and my safety, and I praise You for Your faithful kindness.

44

Now set your heart
and your soul to seek
the Lord your God.

1 CHRONICLES 22:19

ing David wanted to build a house for the God of Israel, but because David was a man of war, the Lord decreed that David's son Solomon would be the builder (1 Chronicles 22:7–9). It was both an enormous task and a great honor. Undoubtedly, Solomon wanted to put forth his best effort. Although David wasn't allowed to build, he was permitted to provide material and workers as well as a verbal commissioning for the tasks (vv. 11–19). David ended his exhortation to Solomon by saying, "Now devote your heart and soul to seeking the LORD your God" (v. 19 NIV). Although none of us will be tasked with the overwhelming responsibility of building a house for the Lord, we will be called to accomplish difficult things and to contribute our skills to edify God's kingdom. In times of stress and in times of ease, we will be wise to devote all we have and everything we are to seeking the Lord.

Father, please teach me to seek You above all things. Help me to commit myself—body and soul and possessions—to honoring You all the days of my life.

45

Let us hold fast
the confession of
our hope without
wavering, for He who
promised is faithful.

HEBREWS 10:23

If you've ever been forced to stand on a crowded subway, there's a good chance you held tightly to one of the rails that run from the ceiling to the floor of the train. Apart from the rails, the sudden starts and stops cause travelers to lose their balance. Holding on to the rail ensures you'll get to your destination safely. In the same way, God's people are called to hold tight to the hope we profess. Practically speaking, the "rails"—the hope—we hold on to in our spiritual lives are the promises of God found in His Word. Life comes at us quickly, and sometimes we are confronted with situations that test our faith. But if we hold tightly to His promises, our faith remains intact because God's Word has the ability to see us through the storms of life. God has a long and faithful history of keeping His promises, and His Word can be trusted.

Father, thank You for the promises You have given me in Your Word. In times of peace and in times of trouble, teach me to cling tightly to those promises and to trust that what You have promised will come to pass.

46

When You said,
"Seek My face,"
My heart said to
You, "Your face,
Lord, I will seek."

PSALM 27:8

It's likely David wrote Psalm 27 before becoming king and during the time when he was being hunted by King Saul and his armies.[11] In those days, David was being pursued by violent men who intended to kill him (v. 12). Despite the stressful conditions, David remained confident and unafraid (vv. 1–3). He didn't try to minimize the seriousness of his situation. Instead he sought the Lord and looked at his circumstances through the lens of faith (vv. 5–6). The key to David's public courage was his private obedience. David took time to seek God and receive guidance from Him. He wrote, "Your face, LORD, I will seek" (v. 8). It wasn't by his own skill or military prowess that David was able to escape the threats of his enemies; rather, it was because he sought the face of the Lord, and thus God delivered him. When troubles come our way, neither should we rely on our own strength. Like David, we should seek the face of the Lord. Then we can enjoy public courage because of our private obedience.

Lord, help me view my troubles through the lens of faith. Let me not depend on my own strength and abilities, but rather depend on You.

47

"Peace I leave with you,
My peace I give to you;
not as the world gives
do I give to you. Let not
your heart be troubled,
neither let it be afraid."

JOHN 14:27

Oftentimes we define *peace* as the absence of turmoil or conflict, but in this context of John 14, that definition is a mischaracterization of the word. When Jesus said to His disciples, just hours before He went to the cross, "Peace I leave with you, My peace I give to you" (John 14:27), He used the word *shalom*, which has a much richer connotation than our typical English rendering of the word *peace*. *Shalom* can be defined as "the notion of a positive blessing, especially as it relates to being in a right relationship with God."[12] In other words, the peace that Christ gives can be experienced even in the midst of hardship or sorrow. Its enjoyment doesn't depend on external circumstances, but stands strong in the harshest conditions. In this way, the peace that comes from Christ differs from the counterfeit peace the world offers. When we realize we can experience God's peace in any situation, our fears are diminished as we entrust our way to the One who is the Way.

> *Jesus, thank You for Your peace that isn't contingent on easy circumstances. When my life is troubled, remind me to seek You so that I may be comforted by Your prevailing peace.*

48

I sought the LORD,
and He heard me,
And delivered me
from all my fears.

PSALM 34:4

Fear can be a blessing if it drives us into the arms of God. When there is money in the bank, and everyone we love is healthy, we tend to disregard our need for God. But when fears overwhelm us and threaten our peace, we are prone to reach out to God—and *that* is a blessing. David wrote, "I sought the LORD, and He heard me, and delivered me from all my fears." As we seek God in faith, He looks back to us and shines upon us (Numbers 6:22–27). When God's face "shines upon" us, it means that He is pleased with us, and He is faithful to extend his grace and mercy.[13] Try as we might, we cannot fully conquer our fears on our own. But if we seek God, He is able to help us in ways that we could never help ourselves.

> *Father, teach me to turn to You when I am fearful. Please give me the strength to continue walking in faithful obedience when I am scared. Overcome my fears with Your presence.*

49

See what great love the
Father has lavished on
us, that we should be
called children of God!
And that is what we are!

1 JOHN 3:1 NIV

In a culture that places a high premium on social status, wealth, appearances, pedigree, and titles, it's tempting to fear we'll fail to measure up. But God has given us the title "children of God" (1 John 3:1). Since we are children of God, our culture doesn't get to define our status. Jesus does. Our worth was settled at Calvary when the sinless Son of God chose to die on our behalf so we could be reconciled to the Father. As recipients of such an act of grace, we have every reason to be the most joyful and thankful people on the planet. Our status as children of God means we have nothing to prove. There is no need for us to strive to climb a social ladder or attempt to show others we measure up. Christians are called to bear fruit with the goal of bringing glory to God rather than ourselves (John 15:5). As people who have nothing to prove, we are free to live productive lives for the glory of God and in service to other people.

> *Lord, I pray I will ignore the status symbols in our culture. Help me to understand that I have nothing to prove because my worth was established by You at Calvary.*

50

Now therefore, I pray,
if I have found grace
in Your sight, show
me now Your way,
that I may know You
and that I may find
grace in Your sight.

EXODUS 33:13

*M*oses was called to lead the Israelites out of the wilderness and into the land of promise (Exodus 3:10). It wasn't an easy assignment. The Israelites were quick to complain and prone to idolatry. But Moses was a man of intercessory prayer, and he sought God on behalf of the people he led. When God instructed Moses to leave Sinai and lead the Israelites toward the land of Canaan (33:1), Moses responded to the command by asking God to accompany them: "If your Presence does not go with us, do not send us up from here (v. 15 NIV). Moses understood that God's presence wasn't to be taken for granted but rather fervently sought. God honored His servant's request. Like Moses, we need to habitually pray for a sense of God's presence and ask Him to teach us His ways so that our relationship with Him grows and we experience Him in our day-to-day living.

> *Father, I ask for a strong sense of Your presence. I pray You will lead and direct my steps. Like Moses, I don't want to go anywhere without You.*

51

"If anyone desires
to come after Me,
let him deny himself,
and take up his cross,
and follow Me."

MATTHEW 16:24

S elf-denial isn't a popular subject, but Jesus spoke of it as a nonnegotiable characteristic for those who follow Him as Lord. Jesus said, "If anyone desires to come after Me, let him deny himself, and take up his cross, and follow Me" (Matthew 16:24). Crucifixion is an eye-opening metaphor for discipleship. What does it mean to "take up our cross"? Christians are called to die to our self-will and take up our cross by embracing God's will and following Jesus no matter the cost.[14] To deny ourselves means to abandon everything in our agenda that doesn't align with God's will. If we follow Jesus as Lord, it means He is the final authority of every aspect of our life. Our personal preferences, hopes, dreams, and plans must defer to God's plan. It's tempting to believe that such a lifestyle might cause unhappiness, but in reality, the opposite is true. The more we follow Christ, the more peace and joy we find in our souls.

Father, teach me to deny myself anything that is contrary to Your will. Give me the desire and the strength to take up my cross and follow You regardless of the cost.

52

I will lift up my eyes
to the hills—
From whence
comes my help?
My help comes
from the LORD,
Who made heaven
and earth.

PSALM 121:1–2

$\mathcal{P}$salm 121 is a Psalm of Ascent. The exact meaning of "Psalm of Ascent" has been debated, but it most likely refers to the songs sung by the Jewish pilgrims who traveled back and forth to Jerusalem to observe the religious feasts.[15] As the traveler approached Jerusalem, he would repeat the words of this psalm. In this era, travel was dangerous, and a pilgrim on foot was confronted with a variety of threats. But the psalmist knew his help came from the Lord. As Christians, all of us have only one keeper. It's tempting to give credit for our provision to another person, our employer, or even ourselves—and many times God does bless us through the providence of other people. But make no mistake, regardless of *how* He provides, our help comes from the Lord. It's appropriate to be grateful to those who help, but we must realize our provision originated with the hand of God.

> *Lord, I acknowledge You as the source of my help, and I thank You for all the ways You provide for me. Wherever my travels take me, help me to always remember You are with me, and I am never alone.*

53

"Before I formed you in
the womb I knew you,
before you were born
I set you apart."

JEREMIAH 1:5 NIV

*E*ven before the prophet Jeremiah was formed in his mother's womb, God possessed complete knowledge of him and had set him apart to preach His Word. God called Jeremiah to be a prophet not just to Israel but to all the nations.[16] That calling was challenging, and Jeremiah was often tasked with delivering a message people didn't want to hear. Knowing God had called him to this role must have reassured Jeremiah when the days were difficult and helped to motivate him to persevere. In the same way, God possessed complete knowledge of each one of us before we were formed in the womb. All those who follow Jesus as Lord have specific works to fulfill while we are on this earth (Ephesians 2:10). We can rest in the assurance that God is all-knowing, and He doesn't call us to any assignment without giving us the ability to fulfill our calling.

> *Father, it's an honor to be known by You, the Most-High God. Please reveal Your calling for my life to me and empower me to complete the work You have given me to do.*

54

The LORD will wait, that He
may be gracious to you;
And therefore He will
be exalted, that He may
have mercy on you.
For the LORD is a
God of justice;
Blessed are all those
who wait for Him.

ISAIAH 30:18

The book of Isaiah reveals that God's people disobeyed the Lord and sought refuge in Egypt. The plan was both rebellious and foolish because the Egyptians had once oppressed the Israelites and thus, in seeking help from Egypt, they were forfeiting their freedom. Sadly, the people of Israel hadn't learned how to wait for the Lord. Instead, they habitually took matters into their own hands. As a result, God disciplined His people to teach them the necessity of waiting on Him, but He did not leave them to languish in His discipline. The prophet Isaiah knew the Lord's character and that He longed to be gracious to His people. When we don't get an answer from God as quickly as we'd like, we too often make our own plans. But God instructs His people to wait on Him. In doing so, we avoid His discipline and reap the benefits of our obedience. Waiting on God is far better than moving forward apart from Him and suffering the consequences of our disobedience.

Father, I thank You for Your grace and compassion. Teach me to wait on You and to live obediently so that I may be blessed.

55

O God, You are my God;

Early will I seek You;

My soul thirsts

for You; . . .

Because Your

lovingkindness is

better than life,

My lips shall praise You.

PSALM 63:1, 3

*P*salm 63 is evidence that God's people can develop confidence during times of trouble. In the opening lines of the psalm, David revealed that he was earnestly seeking God and chose to praise Him in every circumstance (vv. 1, 3). Interestingly, David wrote these words from the wilderness of Judah. It's likely he was fleeing either Saul or Absalom (1 Samuel 23:14–15; 2 Samuel 15:23, 28). In either scenario, David was in trouble. But David mentally rehearsed all the ways God had helped him in the past (Psalm 63:6–7). Rather than complaining about his situation, David chose to offer praise to God and wait in hopeful confidence that the Lord would deliver him again. Remembering all the ways God has worked on our behalf in the past strengthens our faith and encourages us in difficult situations. God doesn't intend for hard conditions to destroy us but rather to make us more confident in His provision.

Lord, there is nothing in this life more satisfying than You. Give me the desire to earnestly seek You all the days of my life and praise You in every circumstance.

56

"If you forgive men
their trespasses, your
heavenly Father will
also forgive you."

MATTHEW 6:14

orgiveness is something many of us struggle with because it is contrary to our nature. Most of us prefer mercy for ourselves and judgment for those who sin against us. But the Bible insists God's people are called to forgive. When Jesus was preaching the Sermon on the Mount, He said, "If you forgive men their trespasses, your heavenly Father will also forgive you" (Matthew 6:14). An unforgiving attitude demonstrates we have a poor understanding of the grace, mercy, and forgiveness the Lord has extended to us. All people have fallen short of the glory of God, and every person needs forgiveness (Romans 3:23). When we are mindful of how much it cost for God to forgive our sins, it makes it much easier to extend forgiveness to those who have hurt us. As recipients of God's mercy, we should be grateful for the grace God has shown us and quick to forgive other people.

> *Father, I thank You for Your forgiveness, and I ask You to help me to be quick to forgive others. I pray grace will be my first response when someone sins against me.*

57

God's judgment is right,
and as a result you will
be counted worthy of
the kingdom of God, for
which you are suffering.

2 THESSALONIANS 1:5 NIV

When Paul wrote his letters to the Thessalonians, he commended them for remaining faithful in the midst of persecution (1 Thessalonians 1:3, 8). This young church was not preoccupied with personal agendas, comfort, or success. They desired to serve the kingdom of God. Paul concluded that the Thessalonians' faith and perseverance in suffering provided evidence of the righteous judgment of God. Paul knew that God was providing the church with the grace it needed to remain steadfast in affliction, and the Lord would continue to work out their sanctification until they were "counted worthy of the kingdom of God" (2 Thessalonians 1:5). Paul's statement doesn't mean they were worthy of their salvation. Salvation is by grace through faith in Christ (Ephesians 2:8–9). Rather, Paul indicated that as God continued to give them the grace to mature spiritually, they would become worthy of the calling they had received (4:1). As we depend on God for salvation, we are equally dependent on Him to help us grow and mature spiritually.

Father, I do not deserve the favor You have given me. But I ask that You sanctify me and make me worthy of the calling I have received.

58

The young lions lack
and suffer hunger;
But those who seek
the Lord shall not lack
any good thing.

PSALM 34:10

$\mathcal{A}$ll of us are driven to pursue things that make us happy. Some of those pursuits might be noble, while others are not. Frequently we believe a relationship, luxury items, social connections, a high-paying job, or recognition in our field of work will fulfill our longings. Although there is nothing wrong with pursuing these things, we are misguided if we think they will ultimately satisfy us. Too often we seek those goals, and when we achieve them, we feel a sense of accomplishment for a time. But then that feeling wears off, and we turn to chasing after the next thing. Time and again we come up empty. That is because, apart from God, there is no lasting satisfaction. Only He can satisfy our deepest longings. If we want lasting fulfillment, the Bible teaches us to seek God rather than worldly pursuits. If we do, the psalmist assures us that we will lack no good thing.

Father, please give me the wisdom to seek You for all my needs. Remind me that the things of the world will ultimately leave me feeling empty, but You provide me with every good thing.

59

"I am the light of the
world. He who follows
Me shall not walk in
darkness, but have
the light of life."

JOHN 8:12

*I*n the gospel that bears his name, the apostle John included a theme of light and darkness, illustrating the differences between the ways of God and the ways of humans. When Jesus came into the world, He brought with Him understanding and illumination of truth that sheds light on the world's darkness.[17] The light repulses people who are entrenched in wrongdoing because it reveals their sinfulness. But Jesus promised that those who follow Him would not be subjected to walking in darkness. John's gospel says, "The light shines in the darkness, and the darkness has not overcome it" (John 1:5 NIV). This world offers only two paths: one leads to darkness, while the way that follows Jesus leads to light. As you lean in to Jesus, you'll find that your path converges more and more with His.

> *Father, I pray that I will walk so closely with Jesus that I will be a light in this dark world. Increase my understanding of Your truth so that I can share it with others.*

60

Every good gift and
every perfect gift is
from above, and comes
down from the Father
of lights, with whom
there is no variation or
shadow of turning.

JAMES 1:17

*H*ave you ever struggled with temptation and wondered about its source? The apostle James insisted that temptation does not originate with God: "Let no one say when he is tempted, 'I am tempted by God'; for God cannot be tempted by evil, nor does He Himself tempt anyone" (James 1:13). James goes on to say that God is the Giver of all good gifts: "Every good gift and every perfect gift is from above, and comes down from the Father of lights" (v. 17). God is worthy of thanksgiving because everything that provides us with comfort, joy, and laughter comes directly from His hand. If you can enjoy a sport, movie, sunset, animal, or relationship, it's because God has imparted the common grace to enjoy His gift. If we were to look around at all the things that give us comfort and happiness, we'd find a reason to praise God every moment of the day.

Father, I thank You because You are the giver of every good gift. I pray that I will be mindful of all Your blessings and that Your praise will continually be on my lips.

61

If someone says, "I
love God," and hates
his brother, he is a liar;
for he who does not
love his brother whom
he has seen, how can
he love God whom
he has not seen?

1 JOHN 4:20

*A*ll people are created in the image of God (Genesis 1:27). So it stands to reason if we love God, we will love people. The apostle John wrote, "If someone says, 'I love God,' and hates his brother, he is a liar" (1 John 4:20). God initiated a relationship with us by loving us first (v. 19). As recipients of that love, God's children should be the most loving people in our communities. Our love for others shouldn't be contingent on their likability or positive qualities. Why? Because it's possible we weren't likable when God first loved us (Romans 5:8). Jesus didn't go to the cross for us because we were likable. He went to Calvary because we were sinners in need of rescue, because it was the Father's will, and because it was a demonstration of His love. Practically speaking, it's wise for us to pray that God will give us a heart of love for other people. But even when we don't "feel it," we must still treat others in a loving way.

> *Father, I pray You will empower me to love people the way You command. Allow me to see others the way You do and love them unconditionally.*

62

For we do not have a
High Priest who cannot
sympathize with our
weaknesses, but was in
all points tempted as
we are, yet without sin.

HEBREWS 4:15

Empathy is a characteristic that helps relationships thrive. When we sense that someone has compassion for our suffering, it builds trust and intimacy. On the other hand, if we suspect someone has no desire to show empathy, there's a good chance we will withdraw. The writer of Hebrews pointed out that, Jesus, our High Priest, can empathize with us in every situation because He was tempted in every way during His time on earth, yet He did not sin. Regardless of the reason for our struggles, Jesus understands our situation. There is no reason to avoid Him or isolate ourselves for fear of being shunned. The Scriptures invite us to approach Jesus in prayer and share exactly how we are feeling. We don't have to hold back or filter what we say because God's people have permission to be transparent with Him in prayer. Jesus both understands our weaknesses and serves as our source of strength to overcome them.

Lord, I am grateful for Your compassion and mercy and understanding. Empower me to give others that same compassion and mercy and understanding that You have poured out on me.

63

Oh, give thanks
to the LORD!
Call upon His name;
Make known His deeds
among the peoples!
Sing to Him, sing
psalms to Him;
Talk of all His
wondrous works!

1 CHRONICLES 16:8–9

When the ark of the covenant was returned to Jerusalem, there was a celebration (1 Chronicles 16). During the commemoration, King David paused to give thanks to the Lord. Although David often sought God during times of trouble, he also worshipped God in times of joy. David began his proclamation of praise by thanking the Lord, and then he called on his listeners to sing psalms to Him and tell of His wonderous works. King David made it a habit of reminding himself, along with those around him, of all the wonderful acts the Lord had done. In times of sadness, worship lifts our spirits and stirs our faith. During times of celebration, worship offers appropriate thanksgiving to God and directs our thoughts to the One who bestows on us every good thing (Psalm 16:2). Worship shouldn't be limited to church services and special occasions but rather should be a part of our everyday vocabulary.

Father, You are worthy of all praise and glory. I pray I will continually rehearse the good deeds You have done. Teach me to be mindful of Your goodness and tell of Your deeds to anyone who will listen.

64

A man's heart
plans his way,
But the LORD directs
his steps.

PROVERBS 16:9

It's wise to make plans and to set goals, but we must remember God is in control of every circumstance. The writer of Proverbs 16 opens with the words, "The preparations of the heart belong to man, but the answer of the tongue is from the LORD" (Proverbs 16:1). God is interested in even the slightest details of our lives, and no plan can succeed apart from His purpose. Even our best efforts will amount to nothing without God's blessing. The psalmist echoes the words of Proverbs: "Unless the LORD builds the house, they labor in vain who build it; unless the LORD guards the city, the watchman stays awake in vain" (Psalm 127:1). No amount of talent, skill, effort, or planning will be fruitful unless God purposes for it to succeed. Self-reliance isn't a positive attribute; God views it as sin. As we make plans, we must prayerfully consult the Lord and seek His guidance.

> *Lord, You are sovereign over all things. I pray You will guide my path and that all my plans will be in alignment with Your will.*

65

And do not be
conformed to this world,
but be transformed by
the renewing of your
mind, that you may
prove what is that good
and acceptable and
perfect will of God.

ROMANS 12:2

If you've ever watched a caterpillar transform into a butterfly, you've seen an ordinary creature transform into a thing of beauty. When Paul wrote the book of Romans, he warned his audience to avoid conforming to this world. Paul was referring to the characteristics of the world that are in contrast to the ways of God. If we aren't careful, the world has the potential to impact our thinking in a negative way. Paul instructed his readers to instead "be transformed by the renewing of your mind" (Romans 12:2). In this context, to be transformed means to change our thinking. The Word of God transforms our minds as we embrace the truth and refuse to conform with thought patterns that are contrary to the Scriptures. As our thought pattern aligns with God's ways, we will be able to discern His will. Like a caterpillar that transforms into a butterfly, our thought life can become a beautiful thing.

> *Lord, I pray You will transform my thinking and equip me to cultivate a thought life that brings me joy and You glory.*

66

"I am the vine, you are the branches. He who abides in Me, and I in him, bears much fruit; for without Me you can do nothing."

JOHN 15:5

*J*esus was the master teacher, and He used illustrations and metaphors that would be instantly familiar to His audience. In first-century Palestine, everyone was familiar with agriculture, so it's not surprising that Jesus used an analogy of a vine and branch to teach the necessity of abiding in Him. The vine nourishes the branch and empowers it to grow and bear fruit. If a branch is detached from the vine, it will quickly decay and become ineffective. That message is just as relevant today, and with it, Jesus provides His followers with exactly what we need to live our lives in a way that brings glory to God. Today, just as then, those who exist apart from Jesus will fail to grow and will follow paths that don't bring glory to God. Being a Christ-follower means we will abide in Jesus all the days of our lives. Only when we are entirely dependent on Him will our lives bear fruit and bring glory to God.

> *Lord, apart from You I can do nothing. Teach me to abide in You so that my life will bear abundant fruit that brings honor to You. Teach me to do my part as I trust You to do Yours.*

67

Bring joy to your
servant, Lord,
for I put my trust in you.
You, Lord, are
forgiving and good,
abounding in love to
all who call to you.

PSALM 86:4–5 NIV

When we are depressed, it's common to reach for something we hope will make us feel better. Temporary remedies might come in the form of food, shopping, entertainment, or any number of things. But how often do we invite God to address our moods? King David was no stranger to melancholy. The Psalms suggest that David struggled with depression, and he continually discussed the topic with the Lord (Psalms 13:2; 42:5). David prayed, "Bring joy to your servant, Lord, for I put my trust in you" (86:4 NIV). As Christians, we have the privilege of bringing all of our anxieties to the Lord in prayer (1 Peter 5:7). It's a mistake to compartmentalize our problems and refrain from addressing our mental and emotional health issues with the Lord. David described God as "abounding in love to all who call to [Him]" (Psalm 86:5 NIV). That love most certainly extends to our emotional, mental, physical, and spiritual health.

Father, thank You for caring about every aspect of my health. I pray for a glad and peaceful mind. Please lead me to the resources and healing I need.

68

Let us therefore come
boldly to the throne
of grace, that we may
obtain mercy and
find grace to help
in time of need.

HEBREWS 4:16

*H*ave you ever dreaded having a conversation with someone because you knew he was going to respond poorly to what you had to say? Have you ever walked on eggshells and avoided speaking openly for fear of how someone would react? Thankfully, that never has to be the case in our prayer life. The book of Hebrews teaches that Jesus has compassion for every situation we find ourselves in. This is possible because, during His time on earth, He was tempted in every way we are, though He did not sin (Hebrews 4:15). With that truth in mind, we are free to confidently approach Him in prayer, with the expectation that He will respond with the mercy and grace we need. Throughout the Scriptures, we repeatedly see God's servants enjoying transparent prayer lives, and they confidently dialogued with God. Close relationships call for open honesty and trust. God provides us with that safe place to speak openly and be heard.

> *Jesus, thank You for the privilege of prayer. I'm grateful that I can come to You, confident that I will receive Your mercy and grace.*

69

Because you have made the
LORD, who is my refuge,
Even the Most High,
your dwelling place,
No evil shall befall you,
Nor shall any plague come
near your dwelling;
For He shall give His
angels charge over you,
To keep you in all your ways.

PSALM 91:9–11

All of us experience things that make us fearful and uncertain about the future. When hard times threaten our peace, we long to have a safe place to turn to that makes us feel secure. For Christians, that "place" is God. The psalmist wrote, "God is our refuge and strength, a very present help in trouble" (Psalm 46:1). As God's beloved children, there is no need to put on a game face and act courageously when we are trembling inside. The Christian life isn't a journey of self-reliance but rather an ongoing dependence on a faithful God. In the midst of hardship, Christ-followers can move forward with confidence, knowing that God will provide in ways we couldn't bring to pass on our own. He even sends His angels to keep evil from us. God's resources are unlimited, and His mercy is great. Regardless of how dismal things seem, God can change our circumstances in the twinkling of an eye and bless us beyond our highest expectations.

> *Father, when I am fearful and worried about what might come, help me focus on You and not my own skills and abilities. Use the difficult times to deepen my faith and increase my trust. I place all confidence in You.*

70

"But the Helper, the
Holy Spirit, whom
the Father will send
in My name, He will
teach you all things,
and bring to your
remembrance all things
that I said to you."

JOHN 14:26

When Jesus gathered with His disciples in the Upper Room just before He went to the cross, the Lord took great care to address their fears and uncertainty. Although the disciples didn't understand what was about to take place, they understood changes were coming, and they were distraught. They had given up everything to follow Jesus and were worried about how they would continue what Jesus had begun. Jesus assured them that He would send the Helper, the Holy Spirit, to guide and teach them and to remind them of everything Jesus had taught them. The Holy Spirit still works in His followers, enabling us to comprehend spiritual truths (1 Corinthians 2:14). It is because of the Spirit's work that we are able to understand the Bible and know truths about God. Every time we read His Word, it's appropriate to ask the Holy Spirit to illuminate the Scriptures and teach us things we couldn't know apart from Him (Psalm 119:18).

Lord, I long to better know You and to better understand Your Word. I pray the Holy Spirit will teach me every time I open the Bible, so that I will grow in wisdom and knowledge of You.

71

If you extend your
soul to the hungry
And satisfy the
afflicted soul,
Then your light shall
dawn in the darkness,
And your darkness shall
be as the noonday.

ISAIAH 58:10

od's people are the beneficiaries of God's grace that leads to our salvation. In light of that truth, as people of God we are called to devote ourselves to serving others. It's God's will for His children to care for the poor and afflicted (Matthew 25:34–36). The prophet Isaiah spoke of caring for the hungry and oppressed. By doing so, our light shines out into the darkness of this world, as bright as the noonday sun. Isaiah continued, "The LORD will guide you continually, and satisfy your soul in drought, and strengthen your bones; you shall be like a watered garden, and like a spring of water, whose waters do not fail" (Isaiah 58:11). As we care for the poor, we can be sure we are in alignment with God's will. Caring for the poor and afflicted is the role of every child of God. If we fail to serve the poor, we not only neglect our role as children of God, we also reject our King (Matthew 25:41–46).

> *Father, please give me a heart for the poor, and guide me in the best way to be quick to meet their needs. Help me to see You in each person I serve.*

72

"My Father's house has many rooms; if that were not so, would I have told you that I am going there to prepare a place for you? And if I go and prepare a place for you, I will come back and take you to be with me that you also may be where I am."

JOHN 14:2–3 NIV

*A*s Jesus prepared to go to the cross, His disciples were anxious about His impending departure and what life would be like in His absence. For three years the disciples had spent all their time with Jesus, and now the cross was imminently approaching. Knowing their fears, Jesus assured them their separation from Him would be temporary. Jesus explained that His Father's house has many rooms, and He was going there to prepare a place for them. One day, they would be reunited and never be separated again. When the trials and tribulations of life get us down, we need to be mindful that a day is coming when we will be in Christ's presence for eternity. What we know in part by faith, we will experience fully as reality. We must remember that the struggles we encounter in this life are only temporary. And, for the Christian, no matter our age, the best days are still to come.

> *Lord, when the trials of this life threaten to discourage me, plant my thoughts firmly on the promised hope of heaven that awaits Your people.*

73

Because you are sons,
God has sent forth the
Spirit of His Son into
your hearts, crying
out, "Abba, Father!"

GALATIANS 4:6

When Jesus spoke of His Father in heaven, He used the Aramaic word *Abba*, which is an intimate term much like the English word *Daddy*.[18] As followers of Jesus Christ, we too have the privilege of referring to the God of the universe as "Abba" (Romans 8:15). Believers are adopted into God's family and thus have all the privileges of sons and daughters of God. The Holy Spirit bears witness with our spirit that we are indeed children of God (v. 16). As dearly loved children, we can approach the throne of our Father with the confidence of a child crawling into her father's lap. Our relationship with God was never intended to be distant or without emotion. Instead, He invites us to experience Him as a loving Father, and He intends to care for us as His well-loved children.

> *Father, thank You for the gift of Your Son and for the privilege of calling You "Abba." I pray my title as "child of God" will always define who I am and guide what I do.*

74

The LORD is near to all
who call upon Him,
To all who call upon
Him in truth.

PSALM 145:18

The Bible insists, "The LORD is near to all who call upon Him, to all who call upon Him in truth" (Psalm 145:18), yet there are times when He feels distant. We cannot allow feelings to dictate our lives. Too often, those feelings are unpredictable and inaccurate. It's possible to get out of bed feeling one way and then feel completely opposite by afternoon. But God's Word doesn't change, and it can always be trusted. If our feelings contradict God's Word, we must choose to believe the Scriptures. Jesus said, "I will never leave you nor forsake you" (Hebrews 13:5). So even when God feels distant or even absent from our lives, the Scriptures promise He is near. We must embrace God's Word by faith and believe that it's true. The apostle Peter wrote, "All flesh is as grass, and all the glory of man as the flower of the grass. The grass withers, and its flower falls away, but the word of the LORD endures forever" (1 Peter 1:24–25).

> *Father, I pray I will rely entirely on You and the promises found in Your Word. Teach me to disregard feelings that hold no truth and rely on Your Word, which never fails.*

75

Trust in the LORD
with all your heart,
And lean not on your
own understanding;
In all your ways
acknowledge Him,
And He shall direct
your paths.

PROVERBS 3:5–6

*T*he book of Proverbs instructs us to trust God "with all your heart" (Proverbs 3:5–6). But sometimes we find ourselves in situations where we don't have a clue about what God is doing. As we look at the events around us, we can't fathom what God is up to, and, if we were in control, we'd certainly do things differently. But the writer of Proverbs instructs us not to rely on our own under-standing. We must remember that God's ways are far greater than our ways: "'For My thoughts are not your thoughts, nor are your ways My ways,' says the LORD. 'For as the heavens are higher than the earth, so are My ways higher than your ways, and My thoughts than your thoughts'" (Isaiah 55:8–9). If we trust that God is good, we don't have to under-stand His plan at every twist and turn. Instead, we must obey Him, trusting that He will lead us on the right path.

Lord, help me to trust You even when I don't understand Your plan. Teach me that I can count on Your love and faithfulness even when I can't see how things will work out.

76

They shall see His face.

REVELATION 22:4

It's possible to be so absorbed in this life that we don't spend any time thinking about eternity. But our relationship with Jesus will outlast our time in this world and will continue in the life to come. One day, we *will* see Him face to face. This is a gift that even Moses, His trusted servant, was denied during his time on this earth (Exodus 33:2–23; 34:29–35). For God's people, a time will come in heaven when our sanctification process will be complete, and the promise of Revelation will be fulfilled: "They shall see His face" (Revelation 22:4). We will behold the face of Christ, and it will be the greatest moment of our existence. Forty billion years from now, very little of what we are experiencing in our present life will matter, but how we cultivate our relationship with Jesus will matter greatly. Let us then be motivated to seek Him today and, by doing so, invest in the life to come.

> Lord, I look forward to the moment when I will finally see You face to face. Teach me to live every moment of this life in anticipation of the next.

77

"My sheep hear My
voice, and I know them,
and they follow Me."

JOHN 10:27

*M*any of us know our parents' voices so well we could pick them out of a million others. When we spend year after year listening to someone speak, it becomes second nature to know the tone, inflections, and most common ways they communicate. In the same way, when we follow Jesus as Lord, we learn to pick His voice out from all the other things that are competing for our attention. The primary ways we come to recognize Jesus' voice are through studying the Scriptures and fellowshipping with Him in prayer. The more we do these things, the better we become at discerning His voice as He speaks to us through His Word and His still, quiet voice. As we learn to distinguish His voice from that of the world, it is helpful to remember that He will never speak anything to us that is contrary to His Word.

Lord, help me to pick Your voice out from among all the others competing for my time and attention. Teach me to desire to hear from You more than any other.

78

In everything give thanks; for this is the will of God in Christ Jesus for you.

1 THESSALONIANS 5:18

*H*ave you ever met someone who complained about everything? Spending time with a chronic complainer is exhausting. Complainers focus on everything that is wrong, while those who are grateful focus on what is right. In the apostle Paul's first letter to the Thessalonians, he wrote, "In everything give thanks" (5:18). Simply put, God's people are commanded to give thanks regardless of the situation. Cultivating an attitude of gratitude takes our thoughts off ourselves and focuses our minds on all the ways God has blessed us. It's appropriate to give thanks to God because He is the source of every good thing we possess (1 Corinthians 4:7). Of course, if there is an area we are lacking, we have permission to ask God to meet those needs (Matthew 7:7–8). But being thankful even as we present our requests stirs our faith by reminding us of all the ways God has already been so good to us.

Father, I pray that words of thanksgiving will flow freely from my mouth and that I will praise You all the days of my life. Help me to focus on all the ways You have already been good to me.

79

"Behold, I stand at the door and knock. If anyone hears My voice and opens the door, I will come in to him and dine with him, and he with Me."

REVELATION 3:20

The book of Revelation contains letters to seven churches. Jesus found no reason to commend the church of Laodicea. They were known for worshipping false idols and willfully rebelling against God. They had prospered financially from a flourishing textile and medical industry and demonstrated in numerous ways they believed they did not need God.[19] Jesus described them as neither hot nor cold and said that because they were lukewarm, He would spit them out of His mouth (Revelation 3:15–16). Jesus called on the church of Laodicea to repent, mourn for their sins, and turn from their sinful ways. Jesus urged the wayward church to allow Him in and to experience His union and fellowship. In much the same way, Jesus still invites individual sinners and those who have strayed from fellowship back to a relationship with Him. Jesus' offer to eat with the repentant church was a symbol of intimacy and a loving relationship.[20] Jesus extends the same offer of a loving relationship to all people today.

> *Lord, I want to live a life that is pleasing to You. I pray I will be quick to repent of the sins in my life that impact my fellowship with You.*

80

Whoever confesses
that Jesus is the Son
of God, God abides in
him, and he in God.

1 JOHN 4:15

If a person recognizes that Jesus is the Son of God, it's because the Holy Spirit has given him or her the ability to perceive this truth (1 Corinthians 2:14). The Bible teaches that the Holy Spirit has been given to believers (Romans 5:5). One of the roles of the Spirit is to teach believers and illuminate the Scriptures so that we grow in understanding of God and the truths about our faith (John 14:26). The apostle Paul prayed for the church at Ephesus, "I pray that the eyes of your heart may be enlightened in order that you may know the hope to which he has called you, the riches of his glorious inheritance in his holy people" (Ephesians 1:18 NIV). As students of God's Word, we always have new things to learn. It's exciting to ponder the reality that the Holy Spirit is our teacher and we can continue to learn from Him and grow in our faith.

Father, I pray the Holy Spirit will teach me new things in Your Word. I ask You to give me a desire to better know You and love Your Scriptures.

81

"For where two or three
are gathered together
in My name, I am there
in the midst of them."

MATTHEW 18:20

God intends for the Christian life to be lived in community; we are not meant to live as "lone rangers." Christ-followers need to be surrounded by their brothers and sisters in Christ. Life is hard, and the Enemy is fierce, and we need other believers' support and encouragement (1 Peter 5:8). Jesus offered another excellent reason for believers to be active participants in biblical communities. He said, "For where two or three are gathered together in My name, I am there in the midst of them" (Matthew 18:20). Jesus declared that He Himself would be present among believers who are seeking unity as they make decisions and as they come together for prayer. In describing the early church, Luke wrote, "They continued steadfastly in the apostles' doctrine and fellowship, in the breaking of bread, and in prayers." (Acts 2:42). To be an active church participant is the precedent that the early church set, and it is necessary today in order for modern-day believers to fully thrive in their faith.

Lord, I thank You for the gift of my brothers and sisters in Christ. I pray You will be present among us as we seek Your will and strive to live in a spirit of unity.

82

Let him who thirsts
come. Whoever
desires, let him take
the water of life freely.

REVELATION 22:17

When Jesus spoke to the woman at the well, He offered her living water and promised that those who drink of it would never thirst again (John 4:10, 14). The metaphor of Christ as living water is one that appears in numerous places in Scripture. The prophet Isaiah wrote, "Come, all you who are thirsty, come to the waters; and you who have no money, come, buy and eat!" (Isaiah 55:1 NIV). Again, in the book of Revelation an invitation is offered to those who are thirsty. Living water is an appropriate metaphor for the person and work of Jesus Christ because it represents a universal need. Without water, our physical bodies perish. In the same way, without Jesus, we are spiritually dead. But Jesus does not leave us to perish. Instead He invites those who are thirsty to drink freely from the fountain of life, and He promises that those who do will never thirst again but will experience eternal life.

> *Father, thank You for the gift of living water. I praise You for the salvation found in the finished work of Jesus Christ.*

83

Good and upright
is the LORD;
Therefore He teaches
sinners in the way.
The humble He
guides in justice,
And the humble He
teaches His way.

PSALM 25:8–9

*H*umility is a characteristic that is sorely lacking in our culture. Our society places such a high premium on individualism that it's not uncommon for people to go to great lengths to make a name for themselves. We're measured by how many people follow us on social media and how many "likes" we get on our postings. But gospel living calls for humility. Jesus said, "Whoever exalts himself will be humbled, and he who humbles himself will be exalted" (Matthew 23:12). Jesus insisted that the humble will not only be exalted but also will be taught and led by God (Psalm 25:9). It takes humility to be teachable. Sadly, some people are more interested in pursuing a platform than a godly character. As Christians, we are not called to make a name for ourselves. We are called to bring glory to the name of our God (John 15:8).

> *Father, help me to humble myself before You, and let the goal of my life be to bring glory to You. Create in me a teachable heart, so that I may learn Your ways and follow Your paths.*

84

And whatever you
do in word or deed,
do all in the name of
the Lord Jesus, giving
thanks to God the
Father through Him.

COLOSSIANS 3:17

There's an old saying that asks, "If you don't have time to do it right, when will you have the time to do it over?"[21] No one respects a task that is half finished or poorly done. That's why the Bible calls for Christians to engage all things with excellence. In Paul's letter to the Colossians, he instructed the church to approach every task as if they were performing it for Jesus. To "do all in the name of the Lord Jesus" (Colossians 3:17) means our labors will be consistent with who Jesus is and what He wants.[22] It doesn't matter if we are taking on a large project at work or scrubbing the floor at home; we should give our greatest effort and do the best job we can. Our best work shows we care and want to contribute something valuable rather than just getting by with the bare minimum.

> *Father, teach me to have an excellent work ethic. Help me to always give my best effort, reminding me that to do my work with dignity shows I care.*

85

"Then you will call
upon Me and go and
pray to Me, and I
will listen to you."

JEREMIAH 29:12

*A*fter God's people were taken captive and exiled to Babylon, the prophet Jeremiah wrote a letter to the surviving exiles. The reason for the letter was to assure them that God had not forgotten them and to instruct them on how to live while they were in captivity (Jeremiah 29:1–10). God commanded they keep being fruitful and productive during their time in captivity and to care about the welfare of the city. They would remain there for seventy years, and then God would bring them home and fulfill the plans He had for them (vv. 10–11). God said, "Then you will call upon Me and go and pray to Me, and I will listen to you" (v. 12). Regardless of our circumstances, God invites us to call on Him and promises to hear our prayers. God didn't forget the exiles, and He hasn't forgotten us. Although sometimes our circumstances don't change as quickly as we'd like, we can trust that God is in control, and His plans are good.

> *Father, I pray that I will be quick to call on You in every circumstance. Teach me to do Your will and to trust Your timing regardless of my current situation.*

86

"Oh, that My people
would listen to Me. . . .
I would soon subdue
their enemies,
And turn My
hand against their
adversaries.

PSALM 81:13–14

*P*salm 81 is a call to worship and to hear God's Word (Psalm 81:1–3, 6–10). As He had done before, God reminded the people of Israel that He had delivered them from the oppression of the Egyptians and led them to the land He promised (vv. 5–6). Sadly, the Israelites refused to listen to His voice, and they rebelled against God (v. 11). As a result, God allowed them to continue in their rebellion and to follow their own path, but their choices soon led to their destruction (vv. 11–12). God then responded, "Oh, that My people would listen to Me. . . . I would soon subdue their enemies, and turn My hand against their adversaries" (vv. 13–14). God is well able to deal with our enemies and set us on the right path, but He insists we listen to His counsel and obey His instruction. When we choose our own way, we are our own worst enemies. Blessings are found only in obeying God and living the way He instructs.

> *Father, give me ears that are quick to hear and obey Your Word. Remove any rebellion from my heart, and lead me on the path of Your righteous will.*

87

And God is able to
make all grace abound
toward you, that you,
always having all
sufficiency in all things,
may have an abundance
for every good work.

2 CORINTHIANS 9:8

*H*uman wisdom conveys the idea that if we want to be wealthy, we must horde the resources we possess and not give anything to others. But the Bible teaches an alternative way of thinking: people of faith are to trust God to provide for our needs. Faith and greed cannot coexist. Christ-followers give freely to meet the needs of others because we serve a God who enthusiastically meets the needs of His people. It's a cycle of sorts; God blesses us so that we can be a blessing. The apostle Paul assured the Corinthian church that God would abundantly bless them and provide everything they needed to give generously to every good work. There isn't a single instance in Scripture where God failed to provide for His people. If God calls us to a task or prompts us to give, He will provide everything we need to obey Him. The children of God have every reason to be the most generous people on the planet.

> *Father, I pray I will serve You and not money. Please remove any hint of greed in me and make me extravagantly generous in meeting the needs of other people.*

88

You were bought at
a price; therefore
glorify God in your
body and in your spirit,
which are God's.

1 CORINTHIANS 6:20

*O*ur culture holds a lax view about sex, and the prevailing attitude is "anything goes." But our culture doesn't define the values of a believer, the Word of God does, and the Scriptures have plenty to say about how we handle our bodies. The phrase, "bought at a price" is an image Paul used in his letter to the church at Corinth, and it's a phrase borrowed from the slave market. As believers, we were purchased with the blood of Christ, and therefore our bodies are no longer our own.[23] The Scriptures instruct believers to flee from sexual immorality. Paul wrote, "Do you not know that your bodies are members of Christ himself? Shall I then take the members of Christ and unite them with a prostitute? Never!" (1 Corinthians 6:15 NIV). Christ-followers are called to bring glory to God with every aspect of who we are, and that includes our bodies.

> *Father, I want to bring glory to You with all of who I am. Because of this, I will honor You with my body, and I will submit to Your lordship in all areas of my life.*

89

The LORD is my rock
and my fortress
and my deliverer;
My God, my strength,
in whom I will trust;
My shield and the
horn of my salvation,
my stronghold.

PSALM 18:2

If a dangerous storm were headed your way, you'd take cover in the safest place in your home. Safety specialists advise going to a center room in the house or underneath a stairwell to experience the greatest protection from inclement weather. No sane person would believe he was strong enough to fight off the destructive forces that come with a powerful storm. In the same way, life sends storms in our direction that are too much for us to handle. David experienced just such a storm when he was hunted by King Saul, who sought to kill him. Saul and his armies were too much for David alone, but David sought refuge in God. As a result, God protected David from Saul's threats, and He delivered him to safety. When we are confronted with outside forces that are too much for us to stand against on our own, we too can seek God as our refuge. We'd be foolish to believe we can save ourselves from everything this world throws at us. We must take refuge in our Lord.

Father, when the storms of life threaten my safety and peace, help me be quick to seek refuge in You. You alone are my Rock and my Deliverer.

90

Since, then, you have
been raised with Christ,
set your hearts on
things above, where
Christ is, seated at
the right hand of
God. Set your minds
on things above, not
on earthly things.

COLOSSIANS 3:1–2 NIV

As believers, few things are more important than understanding our identity in Christ. When Paul wrote to the Colossians, he told them, "You have been raised with Christ" (Colossians 3:1). Paul's words refer to every believer's identification with Christ's death, burial, and resurrection.[24] Because of our identification with Jesus, we have been granted new life, which provides us with the capacity to live differently than we did before. Paul says that since we have been raised with Christ, our minds should be set on things above. Practically speaking, that means we are to think about the things of God. If we aren't intentional about setting our minds on spiritual things, we risk becoming so distracted by the daily demands of our schedule that we don't cultivate our faith life. Paul insists we control and direct our thought processes in such a way that we are preoccupied with God.

Father, I pray You will teach me to "set my mind on things above." Help me focus and control my thoughts in a way that honors You.

91

Beloved, let us love
one another, for love is
of God; and everyone
who loves is born of
God and knows God.
He who does not love
does not know God,
for God is love.

1 JOHN 4:7–8

ove is necessary for God's people. As Christ-followers, we are called to become increasingly more like Jesus. Paul wrote, "For those God foreknew he also predestined to be conformed to the image of his Son" (Romans 8:29 NIV). And if we want to be like Jesus, we must love other people, because that's what He did. The apostle John went so far as to say, "He who does not love does not know God, for God is love" (1 John 4:8). If we struggle with loving other people the way God commands, we need to pray and ask for His help loving others. It is God's will for His children to love both Him and other people (Mark 12:30–31). Asking God to increase our love is a spiritually mature prayer request that aligns perfectly with the Scriptures. It's the type of prayer we can pray in confidence because it seeks to obey God's command to love others the way He loves us (John 13:34).

Father, Your Word says without love I don't know You, and I long to truly know You. I pray You will give me a heart that loves You and other people.

92

"I will never leave you
nor forsake you."

HEBREWS 13:5

A knowledge of God's ongoing presence in our lives provides us with a contentment we won't experience anywhere else. Often, when we lack contentment, we look to material resources to temporarily pacify our restlessness. But the writer of Hebrews warns about this: "Let your conduct be without covetousness; be content with such things as you have. For He Himself has said, 'I will never leave you nor forsake you'" (Hebrews 13:5). Most of us realize that a new purchase won't ultimately fulfill us, but too often we give in to the desire to temporarily fill the void we are experiencing. Rather than looking to money or material possessions to bring us fleeting satisfaction, the Scriptures instruct us to find our contentment in God. Knowing God has promised never to abandon us provides us with the stability we need to enjoy what we already possess. Our contentment will never be found at the mall, online, or in something we can purchase. Contentment is found only in the presence of God.

Father, guide me to seek and find contentment in my relationship with You. Teach me to say no to counterfeit gods that cannot satisfy my real needs.

93

Therefore, if anyone is
in Christ, he is a new
creation; old things
have passed away;
behold, all things
have become new.

2 CORINTHIANS 5:17

All human beings have a history of sin, and many of us have things in our past we are embarrassed by or wish we could do over differently. If the Enemy has his way with us, he will perpetually remind us of those things in our past we are ashamed of and taunt us with our history of sin (Revelation 12:10). But those of us who follow Christ as Lord are not the same people we were before coming to Christ. The apostle Paul wrote, "Therefore, if anyone is in Christ, he is a new creation; old things have passed away; behold, all things have become new" (2 Corinthians 5:17). Christ-followers enjoy a new nature, and as we grow in Christ, we will have new goals, desires, and motivations. Our new nature doesn't mean we won't still struggle with sin, but we will be grieved when we do, and our desire will be for holiness. God is committed to our sanctification process, and the longer we walk with Him, the more like Christ we will become.

Father, thank You for the new nature I have in Jesus Christ. Guide me to grow in my faith and spiritual maturity all the days of my life.

94

If any of you lacks
wisdom, let him ask of
God, who gives to all
liberally and without
reproach, and it will
be given to him.

JAMES 1:5

In our prayer lives, it's not uncommon for us to pray for things like job interviews to go well, good test results, favor with our work, and comfort in this life. There is nothing wrong with praying for these types of things; the Word of God invites us to cast all of our cares on the Lord (1 Peter 5:7). But how often do we ask God for blessings that relate to our spiritual growth and maturity? James instructed his readers, "If any of you lacks wisdom, let him ask of God, who gives to all liberally and without reproach, and it will be given to him" (James 1:5). When we lack knowledge about a situation, we should ask God for wisdom. Most of us aren't asking for too much in our prayer lives. Instead, we are asking for far too little. God gifts His children with wisdom and other priceless gifts, but we need to be people who ask.

> *Father, I pray You will make me wiser than I am and teach me things I couldn't know apart from You. I ask You to give me wisdom in every situation and counsel me in every endeavor.*

95

Therefore we do not lose heart. Even though our outward man is perishing, yet the inward man is being renewed day by day.

2 CORINTHIANS 4:16

*A*s we get older, our bodies don't stay in the same shape they were when we were young. Even if we take excellent care of ourselves, our bodies are impacted by age, and some physical decline is inevitable. Spiritually, however, we have every potential to get stronger with each passing year. The apostle Paul experienced troubles and heartache during his ministry, but he didn't allow himself to be discouraged. Instead he wrote, "Therefore we do not lose heart. Even though our outward man is perishing, yet the inward man is being renewed day by day" (2 Corinthians 4:16). Like everyone else, Paul experienced an aging body, but the older he got, the stronger he became spiritually. As believers, we can look to our older years with great anticipation, because the longer our history with God, the greater our potential to enjoy a vibrant spiritual life with Jesus. Our bodies will age, but we can remain strong in the Lord until He calls us home.

> *Father, I pray I will grow closer to You with each passing year. Help my spiritual fervency to increase so that I will enjoy rich fellowship with You all the days of my life.*

96

Only fear the LORD,
and serve Him in
truth with all your
heart; for consider
what great things He
has done for you.

1 SAMUEL 12:24

S amuel gave a farewell address when he stepped down as judge of Israel and Saul was coronated as king (1 Samuel 12). For years, Samuel had served the Lord faithfully and with integrity (1 Samuel 12:3). In his farewell speech, he recalled many of the ways God had blessed the people of Israel, and he encouraged the people to fear and obey the Lord (1 Samuel 12:13–15). Then Samuel warned of what would happen if the people were disobedient. In every generation, God has been faithful to raise up wise and faithful leaders to serve His people. No leader is perfect, but God uses ordinary people to accomplish extraordinary work for His kingdom. A life of faithful service is a powerful witness to the goodness of God. We don't have to serve in powerful positions to be faithful; we just have to do the work God has assigned us with integrity and perseverance.

> *Father, I pray You will equip me to do the work You have assigned me with integrity and faithfulness. Help me to remember your goodness and bring glory to Your name.*

97

"What man of you,
having a hundred
sheep, if he loses one
of them, does not leave
the ninety-nine in the
wilderness, and go
after the one which is
lost until he finds it?"

LUKE 15:4

I n Luke's gospel, Jesus told a parable about a man who had a hundred sheep, and one of them wandered from the flock and got lost. The shepherd left the ninety-nine sheep to search for the one who was lost. When Jesus told this parable, he was getting a lot of criticism from the Pharisees and the scribes because they had noticed that tax collectors and sinners were drawing near to Jesus (Luke 15:1). But, to their dismay, Jesus declared that there would be more rejoicing in heaven over one sinner who repented than over ninety-nine righteous people who did not need to (v. 7). Jesus told this parable to demonstrate that God cares for prodigals. No person has strayed too far or sinned so greatly that he or she is beyond the grace of God. As God's children, we too are to love prodigals. But more than that, God also intends for us to seek out the lost and introduce them to Jesus and His saving grace.

> *Father, I pray I will have a heart for unbelievers, prodigals, and for those who have lost their way. Use me to tell them of the love of Christ and His unfailing grace.*

98

Jesus said to him, "I am the way, the truth, and the life. No one comes to the Father except through Me."

JOHN 14:6

$\mathcal{I}$ magine if you were diagnosed with a fatal disease, and there was only one medicine that would cure your illness. It's likely you'd go to any length to secure that medicine that would heal you. Spiritually speaking, all human beings were born with a terminal sin problem that separates us from God (Romans 3:23). The only remedy for our sins is the salvation of Jesus Christ. Jesus said, "I am the way, the truth, and the life. No one comes to the Father except through Me" (John 14:6). Some people believe that having only one path to God is narrow-minded and limits their options. But in reality, it's as liberating as a single cure for a terminal illness, except this cure leads to eternal life. Our culture might resist the notion of one path to God, but as people who have been given the cure, we should rejoice that there is a way to be reconciled to our Father.

> Jesus, thank You for providing the cure for my sins. I pray I will live every day with gratitude to You and in anticipation of eternal life with the Father.

99

"Are not two sparrows
sold for a copper
coin? And not one
of them falls to the
ground apart from
your Father's will. . . .
Do not fear therefore;
you are of more value
than many sparrows."

MATTHEW 10:29, 31

*I*n Jesus' day, one copper coin could buy two sparrows, because sparrows were common birds that held little value. But Jesus said that not even one sparrow could fall to the ground without the Father's knowledge. Jesus used this illustration to describe not only God's intimate knowledge of everything that is going on in our lives but also His great love for us. In times of stress, it might be tempting to worry about whether or not God is engaged in our situation or understands our problems. But the Bible assures us that He possesses complete knowledge over all of His creation, and He is not disengaged from our circumstances. If God doesn't permit even a sparrow to fall to the ground apart from His knowledge, He certainly possesses full knowledge of His children. Jesus told us not to fear, because we are worth more than many sparrows. We can rest assured that God is in control, and nothing will be allowed in our life that isn't Father-filtered.

Father, help me remember that You know everything about my circumstances and You have promised never to abandon me. I pray I will be confident in Your provision and trust in Your faithfulness.

100

But to each one of
us grace was given
according to the
measure of Christ's gift.

EPHESIANS 4:7

God's people are recipients of His grace in multiple areas of life. Our salvation is a gift of His grace, as are the ways God gifts His children for service to His kingdom (Ephesians 2:8–9; 4:7). In Paul's letter to the church at Ephesus, he noted that God has blessed individual believers with gifts that will serve the church and build His kingdom. As good stewards of those gifts God has given us, it is our responsibility to utilize and maximize them. Not everyone possesses the same gifts, but each possesses a gift. And God gives us those different gifts in order to serve in a variety of ways and meet diverse sets of needs (Romans 12:6–8; 1 Corinthians 12:8–10). Every believer is equipped to make a significant contribution to the kingdom of God. If we use our gifts well, we will be a blessing to others and bring glory to God.

> *Father, I pray I will be an excellent steward of the gifts and the grace You have given me. Help me to use my gifts to serve others and to bring You glory.*

Notes

Chapter 9

1. ESV *Study Bible* (Wheaton, IL: Crossway, 2007), 2273, footnote.

Chapter 10

2. Wayne Grudem, *Systematic Theology: An Introduction to Biblical Doctrine* (Grand Rapids: Zondervan, 2000), 1253.

Chapter 18

3. David Allan Hubbard, *Tyndale Old Testament Commentaries: Hosea* (Downers Grove, IL: InterVarsity Press, 2009), 133.

Chapter 19

4. D. Martyn Lloyd-Jones, *Studies in the Sermon on the Mount* (Grand Rapids: William B. Eerdmans, 1959–1960), 65.

Chapter 25

5. ESV *Study Bible* (Wheaton, IL: Crossway, 2007), 2122, footnote.

Chapter 26

6. Bruce K. Waltke, *The Book of Proverbs, Chapters 15–31* (Grand Rapids: William B. Eerdmans, 2005), 11.

Chapter 29

7. ESV *Study Bible* (Wheaton, IL: Crossway, 2008), 1729, 1739, notes/footnotes.

Chapter 35

8. Warren W. Wiersbe, *Be Alert (2 Peter, 2 & 3 John, Jude): Beware of Religious Imposters* (Colorado Springs: David C. Cook, 1984), 23–24.

Chapter 38

9. ESV *Study Bible* (Wheaton, IL: Crossway, 2007), 976, footnotes.

Chapter 41

10. Warren W. Wiersbe, *Be Worshipful (Psalms 1–89): Glorifying God for Who He Is* (Colorado Springs: David C. Cook, 2004), 235–238.

Chapter 46

11. Wiersbe, *Be Worshipful*, 107–108.

Chapter 47
12. ESV *Study Bible* (Wheaton, IL: Crossway, 2007), 2053, footnote.

Chapter 48
13. Wiersbe, *Be Worshipful*, 107–108.

Chapter 51
14. ESV *Study Bible* (Wheaton, IL: Crossway, 2008), 1842, footnote.

Chapter 52
15. Craig C. Broyles, *Psalms: Understanding the Bible Commentary Series* (Grand Rapids: Baker Books, 1999), 445.

Chapter 53
16. ESV *Bible* (Wheaton, IL: Crossway, 2001), 1369, footnote.

Chapter 59
17. R. C. Sproul, *John: St. Andrew's Expositional Commentary* (Sanford, FL: Reformation Trust Publishing, 2009), 156.

Chapter 73
18. Max Anders, *Holman New Testament Commentary: Galatians, Ephesians, Philippians, & Colossians* (Nashville: Holman Reference, 1999), 56.

Chapter 79

19. ESV *Study Bible* (Wheaton, IL: Crossway, 2007), 2668, footnote.

20. John MacArthur, *Revelation 1–11: The MacArthur New Testament Commentary* (Chicago: Moody Publishers, 1999).

Chapter 84

21. John Wooden, "Quotes," *Goodreads.com*, accessed November 13, 2018, https://www.goodreads.com/quotes/214844-if-you-don-t-have-time-to-do-it-right-when.

22. John MacArthur, *Colossians & Philemon: The MacArthur New Testament Commentary* (Chicago: Moody Publishers, 1992), 160.

Chapter 88

23. ESV *Study Bible* (Wheaton, IL: Crossway, 2008), 2199, footnote.

Chapter 90

24. Anders, *Galatians,* 326.

My Favorite Bible Verses

....

....

....

....

....

....

....

....

....

....

....

....

....

....